SOCIAL ENTREPRENEURSHIP

THE ART OF MISSION-BASED VENTURE DEVELOPMENT

WILEY NONPROFIT LAW, FINANCE, AND MANAGEMENT SERIES

The Art of Planned Giving: Understanding Donors and the Culture of Giving by Douglas E. White

Beyond Fund Raising: New Strategies for Nonprofit Investment and Innovation by Kay Grace

Budgeting for Not-for-Profit Organizations by David Maddox

Charity, Advocacy, and the Law by Bruce R. Hopkins

The Complete Guide to Fund Raising Management by Stanley Weinstein

The Complete Guide to Nonprofit Management by Smith, Bucklin & Associates

Critical Issues in Fund Raising edited by Dwight Burlingame

Developing Affordable Housing: A Practical Guide for Nonprofit Organizations, Second Edition by Bennett L. Hecht

Financial and Accounting Guide for Not-for-Profit Organizations, Fifth Edition by Malvern J. Gross, Jr., Richard F. Larkin, Roger S. Bruttomesso, John J. McNally, PricewaterhouseCoopers LLP

Financial Management for Nonprofit Organizations by Jo Ann Hankin, Alan Seidner, and John Zietlow

Financial Planning for Nonprofit Organizations by Jody Blazek

The Fund Raiser's Guide to the Internet by Michael Johnston

Fund-Raising: Evaluating and Managing the Fund Development Process, Second Edition by James M. Greenfield

Fund-Raising Fundamentals: A Guide to Annual Giving for Professionals and Volunteers by James M. Greenfield

Fund-Raising Regulation: A State-by-State Handbook of Registration Forms, Requirements, and Procedures by Seth Perlman and Betsy Hills Bush

Grantseeker's Toolkit: A Comprehensive Guide to Finding Funding by Cheryl S. New and James Quick

High Performance Nonprofit Organizations: Managing Upstream for Greater Impact by Christine Letts, William Ryan, and Allen Grossman

Intermediate Sanctions: Curbing Nonprofit Abuse by Bruce R. Hopkins and D. Benson Tesdahl

International Fund Raising for Nonprofits by Thomas Harris

International Guide to Nonprofit Law by Lester A. Salamon and Stefan Toepler & Associates

The Law of Fund-Raising, Second Edition by Bruce R. Hopkins

The Law of Tax-Exempt Healthcare Organizations by Thomas K. Hyatt and Bruce R. Hopkins

The Law of Tax-Exempt Organizations, Sixth Edition by Bruce R. Hopkins

The Legal Answer Book for Nonprofit Organizations by Bruce R. Hopkins

A Legal Guide to Starting and Managing a Nonprofit Organization, Second Edition by Bruce R. Hopkins

Managing Affordable Housing: A Practical Guide to Creating Stable Communities by Bennett L. Hecht, Local Initiatives Support Corporation, and James Stockard

Managing Upstream: Creating High-Performance Nonprofit Organizations by Christine W. Letts, William P. Ryan, and Allan Grossman

Nonprofit Boards: Roles, Responsibilities, and Performance by Diane J. Duca

Nonprofit Compensation and Benefits Practices by Applied Research and Development Institute International, Inc.

The Nonprofit Counsel by Bruce R. Hopkins

The Nonprofit Guide to the Internet, Second Edition by Michael Johnston

Nonprofit Investment Policies: A Practical Guide to Creation and Implementation by Robert Fry, Jr.

The Nonprofit Law Dictionary by Bruce R. Hopkins

Nonprofit Compensation, Benefits, and Employment Law by David G. Samuels and Howard Pianko

Nonprofit Litigation: A Practical Guide with Forms and Checklists by Steve Bachmann

The Nonprofit Handbook, Second Edition: Volume I—Management by Tracy Daniel Connors

The Nonprofit Handbook, Second Edition: Volume II—Fund Raising by Jim Greenfield

The Nonprofit Manager's Resource Dictionary by Ronald A. Landskroner

Nonprofit Organizations' Business Forms: Disk Edition by John Wiley & Sons, Inc.

Partnerships and Joint Ventures Involving Tax-Exempt Organizations by Michael I. Sanders

Planned Giving: Management, Marketing, and Law by Ronald R. Jordan and Katelyn L. Quynn

Private Foundations: Tax Law and Compliance by Bruce R. Hopkins and Jody Blazek

Program Related Investments: A Technical Manual for Foundations by Christie I. Baxter

Reengineering Your Nonprofit Organization: A Guide to Strategic Transformation by Alceste T. Pappas

Reinventing the University: Managing and Financing Institutions of Higher Education by Sandra L. Johnson and Sean C. Rush, PricewaterhouseCoopers LLP

The Second Legal Answer Book for Nonprofit Organizations by Bruce R. Hopkins

Special Events: Proven Strategies for Nonprofit Fund Raising by Alan Wendroff

Strategic Communications for Nonprofit Organizations: Seven Steps to Creating a Successful Plan by Janel Radtke

Strategic Planning for Nonprofit Organizations: A Practical Guide and Workbook by Michael Allison and Jude Kaye, Support Center for Nonprofit Management

Streetsmart Financial Basics for Nonprofit Managers by Thomas A. McLaughlin

A Streetsmart Guide to Nonprofit Mergers and Networks by Thomas A. McLaughlin

Successful Marketing Strategies for Nonprofit Organizations by Barry J. McLeish

The Tax Law of Charitable Giving by Bruce R. Hopkins

The Tax Law of Colleges and Universities by Bertrand M. Harding

Tax Planning and Compliance for Tax-Exempt Organizations: Forms, Checklists, Procedures, Third Edition by Jody Blazek

The Universal Benefits of Volunteering: A Practical Workbook for Nonprofit Organizations, Volunteers and Corporations by Walter P. Pidgeon, Jr.

The Volunteer Management Handbook by Tracy Daniel Connors

OTHER TITLES IN THE *Mission-Based Management Series* by Peter C. Brinckerhoff

Faith-Based Management: Leading Organizations That Are Based on More Than Just Mission

Financial Empowerment: More Money for More Mission

Mission-Based Management: Leading Your Not-for-Profit into the 21st Century

Mission-Based Marketing: How Your Not-for-Profit Can Succeed in a More Competitive World

SOCIAL ENTREPRENEURSHIP

THE ART OF MISSION-BASED VENTURE DEVELOPMENT

PETER C. BRINCKERHOFF

JOHN WILEY & SONS, INC

New York • Chichester • Weinheim • Brisbane • Singapore • Toronto

Copyright © 2000 by John Wiley & Sons, Inc. All rights reserved.

Published simultaneously in Canada.

This publication is designed to provide accurate and authoritative information in regard to the subject matter covered. It is sold with the understanding that the publisher is not engaged in rendering legal, accounting, or other professional services. If legal advice or other expert assistance is required, the services of a competent professional person should be sought.

Library of Congress Cataloging-in-Publication Data:

Brinckerhoff, Peter C., 1952–
    Social entrepreneurship : the art of mission-based venture development / Peter C. Brinckerhoff.
       p.   cm. — (Wiley nonprofit law, finance, and management series)
    Includes bibliographical references and index.
    ISBN 0-471-36282-4 (cloth: alk. paper)
    1. Issues management.   2. Nonprofit organizations—Management.   3. Associations, institutions, etc.—Management.   I. Title.   II. Series.
    HD59.5 .B75 2000
    658′.048—dc21

                                                   99-058144

Printed in the United States of America.

10 9 8 7 6 5 4 3 2 1

For all the risk takers,
and especially for my father-in-law,
Luke Hargroves (1919–2000),
who took the ultimate risk for all of us
65 times in the skies over Europe
1943–1945

Contents

Chapter 8   Applying the Lessons: A Step-by-Step Business-Planning Exercise   / 117

Chapter 9   Financing Your Entrepreneurship   / 147

Chapter 10   Technicalities: Unrelated Business Income Tax and Corporate Structuring   / 175

Chapter 11   Social Entrepreneurism for Funders   / 201

Chapter 12   Final Thoughts   / 215

About the Author

Peter Brinckerhoff is an internationally acclaimed consultant, author, and lecturer. He is president of Corporate Alternatives, inc., the consulting firm that he founded in 1982. He is a former staff member, executive director, board member, and volunteer for local, state, and national not-for-profit organizations.

Peter is the author of four other books: *Mission-Based Management: Leading Your Not-For-Profit into the 21st Century; Financial Empowerment: More Money for More Mission; Mission-Based Marketing: How Your Not-For-Profit Can Succeed in a More Competitive World;* and *Faith-Based Management: Leading Organizations That Are Based on More Than Mission.*

Peter lives in Springfield, Illinois, with his wife and three children.

Acknowledgments

For this book I again have two editors to thank. Bob Follett, my good and true friend, and the editor of my first three books, saw potential in my early drafts, pointed me toward it, and provided me insights in how to give you, the reader, more value. Martha Cooley, of John Wiley & Sons, provided much needed counsel on the strategy for the book and how to appeal to a wider audience. Both of them deserve my thanks, and I give it wholeheartedly.

Andy Souerwine, a lifelong friend as well as Professor Emeritus of Management and Organization at the School of Business Administration at the University of Connecticut, also cast his wise eye over the manuscript early in the process. His ideas and observations were invaluable in helping me focus on better ways to teach you the business development process that is so integral to your becoming a social entrepreneur.

After you read the book, if you like what you see, remember that most of the good stuff here is in large portion due to Andy, Bob, and Martha. Blame the bad stuff on me.

SOCIAL ENTREPRENEURSHIP

THE ART OF MISSION-BASED VENTURE DEVELOPMENT

1

Introduction

OVERVIEW

In this chapter you will learn about the following:

➤ The Need for Social Entrepreneurs in a Mission-Based Organization
➤ The Intended Audience for This Book
➤ The Benefits of Reading This Book
➤ Chapter-by-Chapter Overview
➤ How to Get the Most from This Book

A. THE NEED FOR SOCIAL ENTREPRENEURS IN A MISSION-BASED ORGANIZATION

Social entrepreneurs are different, and every not-for-profit organization needs them. Social entrepreneurs are *people who take risk on behalf of the people their organization serves.* Traditional entrepreneurs take risk on their own behalf, or on the behalf of their company's *stockholders.* In not-for-profits the risks are taken on behalf of the *stakeholders.* That difference is significant, and it all comes back to mission. The reason you, your staff, and board take entrepreneurial risks is to get more mission out the door, sooner, better, and in a more focused manner.

Social entrepreneurship is one of the essential characteristics of successful not-for-profits. Social entrepreneurs have the following characteristics that we will discuss at great length in Chapter 2, The Benefits of the Social Entrepreneurism Model.

They are constantly looking for new ways to serve their constituencies and to add value to existing services.

They are willing to take reasonable risk on behalf of the people that their organization serves.

They understand the difference between needs and wants.

1

They understand that all resource allocations are really stewardship investments.

They weigh the social and financial return of each of these investments.

They always keep mission first, but know that without money, there is no mission output.

Being a social entrepreneur is increasingly important as the environment for the charitable sector becomes more and more competitive for donated dollars, traditional grants and contracts, and even for quality staff and volunteers.

While social entrepreneurs can and should take risks, as stewards of their not-for-profits, they should make sure that those risks are reasonable. Thus the need for the business-planning and development skills and techniques that will be covered in the following chapters. The use of for-profit business techniques in the not-for-profit environment is an accelerating reality in most parts of the philanthropic sector. It probably is in your area of service as well, and that may be why you have chosen to read this book.

But being "businesslike" is still controversial in a mission-based organization. Does your organization really need business development skills, even though it is a not-for-profit? *Absolutely.* For far too long, mission-based organizations have suffered under the illusion that they, as charitable organizations, don't need anything from the business world. *"We're different,"* I've heard a thousand, perhaps 10,000, times, *"We are about our mission, not about money. Using business techniques is totally inappropriate. I wouldn't even consider it."*

Let me count the ways that this perception is inaccurate, outdated, and harmful to your organization's ability to do your mission more effectively in increasingly competitive times.

First, your organization already is a mission-based *business*.   You need to think of your entire organization as a business "with a heart," as one client of mine puts it, but one that is businesslike, uses business techniques to pursue its mission, and worries about the bottom line, both in terms of finance and mission. You are in the business of doing mission, not solely making money, but you are *not* a charity. Later in the book we'll discuss return on investment—a very businesslike concept—but one that we will focus on in terms of mission return. You see, you can use business ideas, business concepts, and business techniques to further your mission. Being businesslike can and should increase your capacity to do excellent mission, it should not in any way reduce your capacity to care, your concern for your community, or your humanity as an individual or an organization.

Second, you are a steward.   Whether you are a paid staff member or a volunteer, you are a steward of the resources of your organization. You are charged with getting the most mission you can out of the resources at hand, and, as I pointed out earlier, some of those resources are business techniques. Wouldn't you use a grant from a foundation to do something needed in your community (if you could do it well)? Of course you would! Then why wouldn't you adopt good marketing practices to do more mission? Or do good cash flow analysis, or practice good property management, good human resources techniques, inventory management, investment strategies, or any of the hundreds of other business practices that are available to you for the asking? If you turn away from these resources, you are simply *not* doing your job as a steward.

Third, the world has changed.   Businesses, at least the successful ones, know how to compete. They figure out who their target markets are, ask those markets what they want, and give it to them as best they can. They focus on their core competencies and cast off what they cannot do well. They focus on customer satisfaction, not just on customer service. They improve 1 percent a day, every single day of the year. Everyone in their organization is on the marketing team. They know who their competition is in every single arena, and they pay attention to what their competition does. They know every one of their costs and work to contain them. You and your organization are in an era that is more competitive, and less forgiving, and to survive and thrive, business techniques are essential. You are competing much more actively for donated dollars, quality staff and volunteers, and, in many cases, people to serve. You are expected to quantify your outcomes and be more accountable to the governments, foundations, insurers, and donors that provide you with the funds you need to provide your mission.

Now what about you? Are you still thinking of yourself as a charity? If so, you are way, way behind the curve. You need to discard the old ways of thinking (as I suspect you probably have because you are reading this) and adapt to the changing environment, the new reality.

If the preceding description of the successful organization sounds like your organization, great! You've made a good start and will hone your skills by going through these pages. If it doesn't, perhaps there are some ideas you can garner from the remainder of the book.

In the following pages, I'll show you the skills you need to become a social entrepreneur and help your organization survive and thrive in this new and increasingly hectic environment. I'll show you how to use business development skills to focus on what your community wants and needs, how to match those wants with your core competencies, how to develop new project ideas, test their feasibility, and then write a business plan. We'll cover how to find money for your business and how to project finances in the plan. And, we'll go over some very technical issues as well, such as the Unrelated Business Income Tax and the myriad of corporate structuring options that you may want to use to house your business.

Becoming a social entrepreneur is not easy. It is not without risk, as you will see. But the skills and techniques I show you here are a method of assessing risk and gauging opportunity that can strengthen your organization, make your job as a mission-based manager more interesting and productive, and, ultimately, lead to more and better services for the people you serve. Not bad outcomes at all.

I hope that you are not just reading this book to develop one business and have it segregated from the rest of your not-for-profit. What I want you to do is to develop the idea of social entrepreneurship throughout your organization, and then to use business skills to further all parts of your mission. The skill of developing new businesses is just one of many such business-related capabilities that will help you and your organization. To eschew the idea that business can be good mission is, in the end, harmful to the mission capability of your organization.

B. THE INTENDED AUDIENCE FOR THIS BOOK

This book is specifically written for staff members, policy setters, and volunteers of mission-based organizations. No matter which of these important roles you fill, you will find information and ideas that you can put to immediate and mission-beneficial use in the following pages. Please don't limit the circulation of this text to just your policy-setting staff and volunteers. I hope that your social entrepreneur team will include people from throughout your organization, line staff, middle managers, and members of your senior management team. Similarly, volunteers from finance, marketing, services, and, of course, your board of directors may all have perspectives and input into the business-planning process, and thus will get value from the book.

There are several reasons why you might be considering reading this book. And, as you think through whether it is worth your time, let me list a few situations that could benefit from learning about social entrepreneurism.

1. You are considering expanding current services to a new community or county, or to a new population.

2. You are considering expanding the volume of services you provide. For example, a key funder comes to you with a potential expansion of an existing grant or contract.

3. You are considering establishing a completely new service, inside or outside of your current service area.

4. You are considering a collaboration with another organization.

If any or all of these sound familiar, this book has much to offer you, since you can apply the tenets of social entrepreneurism to them and make better mission decisions. You will learn a lot in these pages that will help you if these situations confront you.

C. THE BENEFITS OF READING THIS BOOK

What will you learn and how will you benefit from your investment of time? In at least the following ways:

1. You will learn how to be a social entrepreneur and how to develop or improve your business development skills, which in turn will make you a better manager in pursuit of your mission.

2. You will learn how social entrepreneurship can benefit your organization *even if you never develop an outside business.*

3. You will better understand the concept of needs and wants and how essential this concept is to the provision of high-quality services.

4. You will know more about return on investment—both financial and social. You will look on resource allocation as an investment, not as an expenditure.

5. You will know how to go through the entire business development process in a way that minimizes your risk and maximizes your mission outcome.

6. You will increase the likelihood that your organization can and will continue to survive and thrive in an increasingly competitive era.

There is much more, of course: examples, hands-on ideas, and some sample feasibility studies and business plans. I promise you that you will come away from this book both empowered and excited about quickly applying what you've learned to your day-to-day, month-to-month, and year-to-year mission provision. To help you as you navigate through the book, let's next examine how I've organized the materials.

D. CHAPTER-BY-CHAPTER OVERVIEW

This book is divided into 12 chapters. Each chapter is set up to help you receive the most benefit from your reading. Let's go over the features that you will find in every chapter. First, you will find an **OVERVIEW,** which is a brief summary of the major subjects that I will cover in the chapter. In the body of the chapter you will find two other features. ❏ **FOR EXAM-PLE** will indicate a story or short example from the not-for-profit or business world. These examples are designed to illustrate a point or an idea in the text. The ☞ **HANDS-ON** symbol is good news for readers who want ideas that they can immediately use; it means that just such a suggestion will be provided for you. The intent is to help you apply what you have just learned and give you a hint, idea, or gentle nudge to get you started.

At the end of each chapter are two additional features. The first is a **RECAP,** in which I review the key ideas that I provided you, as a reminder and summary. The final section of each chapter is entitled QUESTIONS FOR DISCUSSION, and it provides you with a number of questions that you can use with your fellow staff and/or volunteers to analyze the uses and impacts of the ideas that are contained in the chapter.

Now that you know the design of the individual chapters, let's look at their sequence and content.

> **Chapter 1, Overview.**   This is the chapter you are reading now. It provides a short discussion of why business development skills are so crucial in a mission-based organization, what comprises business development, who the book is written for, a listing of the benefits I promise to deliver as you read the book, a short description of the contents of each chapter, and some ways that I recommend to assure that you get the most out of the book.

> **Chapter 2, The Benefits of the Social Entrepreneurship Model.**   In this chapter I will start by defining the many activities that I feel qualify as social entrepreneurship. You will see that it goes far beyond just starting up a new service or outside business. Then, we'll lay the groundwork for your business development efforts. I know from helping hundreds of not-for-profits develop businesses that you will run into people (on your board, your staff, or from your funders) who disagree with your intent to develop or expand a business. This chapter will help, as I will lay out some very specific rationales for business development, including the benefits to your organization and the people you serve. I will also take a look at the downside of not using the model and give you some examples of the potential grief people come to.

> **Chapter 3, The Business Development Process.**   In this chapter we'll detail the seven essential steps of the not-for-profit business development process. These steps are not the same as those used by for-profit organizations, and we will go through them as a group and

individually to give you an overview of the process and why it is so important not to skip steps. Finally, I'll provide you with a self-assessment tool to see if your organization is ready for social entrepreneurism.

Chapter 4, First Steps: Mission Outcomes, Risk, and Idea Generation. Once we have gone through the seven steps, we will begin to go through them in great detail. In this chapter, we'll talk about mission outcomes, the concept of risk in the mission-based organization, and how you start to generate your ideas for new businesses or services.

Chapter 5, Feasibility Studies. You need to walk before you can run, and you need to determine feasibility before you spend the time and money developing a full business plan. In this chapter, we'll talk through why you should look at project feasibility and how to do so by writing a preliminary and then a final feasibility study. I'll show you the questions to ask and the places to find the information you need to answer them.

Chapter 6, The Business Plan. The business plan is the heart and soul of the process, and this chapter will show you why you should write one (even after all the feasibility work makes the project look good), what you should include in a business plan, and how you should go about setting your goals and objectives for the plan.

Chapter 7, Business Plan Financial Projections. The thing your board, staff, volunteers, and funders will want to see the most in your plan is your financials, and this chapter will give you the tools and formats you need to do them right. We'll start by giving you some common financial projection mistakes to avoid. Then we'll walk through the essential financial projections that your plan will need, including income and expense projections, cash flow estimates, start-up costs, breakeven analysis, and return on investment.

Chapter 8, Applying the Lessons: A Step-by-Step Business-Planning Exercise. Now you get to apply what you have learned. This is really a fill-in-the-blanks chapter, with forms and formats for you to apply immediately. Be sure to make copies of this chapter, as you will want to use the forms many times.

Chapter 9, Financing Your Entrepreneurship. Now that you have your business plan in hand, where will you get the money to start and run the business? In this chapter, we'll review the places that your organization can seek funding, the different ways you can go about it, and some rules for financing that will keep both your costs and your stress levels to a minimum.

Chapter 10, Technicalities: Unrelated Business Income Tax and Corporate Structuring.   There are some technical things to consider beyond your financing when contemplating business development. This chapter will cover the two most common ones: the Unrelated Business Income Tax (UBIT), and uses of corporate structuring for your business. I'll show you how to determine your UBIT status and how to determine the best corporate configuration to meet your mission needs.

Chapter 11, Social Entrepreneurism for Funders.   This chapter is specifically focused for those who fund a huge percentage of the not-for-profit sector: government, United Way, foundations, and corporations. There are things that those who pay can do to foster social entrepreneurs, and other things that they must do to assure high-quality services remain in an entrepreneurial environment. I'll show you both in this chapter, and I will try to convince the funders that social entrepreneurism is a good thing for everyone.

Chapter 12, Final Thoughts.   Social entrepreneurism can help make your organization more mission-capable, can focus you on being market-driven and still mission-based, and can help you provide better services sooner to the people that depend on you in your community. It can also distract you, steer you away from your core values, and wind up bankrupting you. In this all-important final chapter, I'll show you the warning signals, how to avoid running your organization aground because you weren't paying attention to the charts and forgot that there were rocks out there. We'll look at ways to stay focused on your mission and to make sure that mission, not just money, is the end product of the process.

Resources for Further Study.   This section includes a number of sources for business development assistance, training, and some Internet sites.

I'm sure that it sounds like a lot to cover, and I am sure you are both excited and a little apprehensive about starting to plow through it. With all that reading ahead, it makes sense to stop here and take a moment to think through how to go through the book efficiently and effectively.

E. HOW TO GET THE MOST FROM THIS BOOK

Let's look at the ways that you and your staff and volunteers can get the most from reading this book. Again, I want you to get the highest level of return from your investment of time and money.

First, read the book through in the order that it is written. I know that if you are like most readers, you have certain areas, such as feasibility studies, finance, or how to convince your funders, that you are most interested in, but I urge you to read the book in order. I wrote the chapters in this order for a reason: They build on each other, each subject leading to the next. Try to avoid moving back and forth, and read it through once from cover to cover. Then, if you want to, you can reread the parts that you need to focus on the most at a later time. If you don't read the book through, you run the risk of learning about just the issues that you feel you are short on, and not taking a look at areas in which you may have an organizational blind spot.

Second, read the book as a team, if you can. Read a chapter, pass it around to your social entrepreneur team and then use the questions at the end of each chapter to talk through ways to implement the ideas in each section. If you can afford to, buy multiple copies so that you can expedite the process. If you can't, fine. It will take a little more time, but going through the book as a group insures you will give all of my ideas a more complete examination, and it can build consensus for any changes that you may find are needed.

RECAP

In this initial chapter, you've learned why social entrepreneurs are crucial to the success of any not-for-profit organization. We briefly covered how quickly the world is changing and how good stewards are willing to exhibit the key characteristic of the social entrepreneur: the willingness to take risks on behalf of others, the people your organization serves.

Then, you learned more about this book and how to get the most out of it. I outlined the six major benefits of reading the book, gave you a summary of each chapter, and then provided some suggestions on how to get the most out of our time together.

In the following chapters, you will put this information to good use. Our first job is to define what a social entrepreneur is in more detail and how to link entrepreneurism with traditional business planning. That's the subject of our next chapter.

2

The Benefits of the Social Entrepreneurism Model

OVERVIEW

In this chapter you will learn about the following:

➤ Defining Social Entrepreneurism
➤ The Link between Social Entrepreneurism and Business Development
➤ The Uses of Social Entrepreneurism to Do More Mission
➤ The Benefits to the Organization
➤ The Risks of Not Using the Model

You already have a lot to do: budgeting, supervision, dealing with the board, the community, your funders. You even provide services! So why would you want to take the time to make the changes needed to develop a new business? Why learn about social entrepreneurism and its close cousin, new business development? Why invest in this, instead of some other focus?

That's what we'll talk about in this chapter. First, we'll start at the beginning: my definition of social entrepreneurism. I'll show many uses for the social entrepreneurism model, and then how you can use business development to benefit your organization, your constituency, and your community. Finally, we'll look at the risk you run of not using a social entrepreneurism strategy in your organization. While you may already be convinced you need to make this transition, others in your organization may not be as enlightened. This chapter will help you convince them.

A. DEFINING SOCIAL ENTREPRENEURISM

Social entrepreneurism. A long, tongue-twister of a term. But what does it mean? To me the core of social entrepreneurism is good stewardship.

Good stewards don't just rest on their laurels, they try new things, serve people in new ways, are lifelong learners, try to have their organizations be fonts of excellence. Social entrepreneurs have these characteristics:

They are constantly looking for new ways to serve their constituencies and to add value to existing services.

They are willing to take reasonable risk on behalf of the people that their organization serves.

They understand the difference between needs and wants.

They understand that all resource allocations are really stewardship investments.

They weigh the social and financial return of each of these investments.

They always keep mission first, but know that without money, there is no mission output.

These are crucial traits for you to mull over as you consider your organizational adaptation to the social entrepreneurism model. How do you, your staff, and board view risk? As something to avoid, or as something that is part of steady improvement of services to the community? What about services? Are you doing the same old thing you were five years ago, or can you specifically list what the organization did to improve services last week, the week before that, and the week before that? Steady, consistent improvement in services and the constant adding to the value of those services from the point of view of the people you serve and the people who pay for them is an absolute necessity if you are to become and remain a social entrepreneur.

Budgeting as investment is another concept that entrepreneurs are comfortable with. When you allocate staff, property, or cash to an issue or a project, it is really an investment in that part of your mission. But is it a good one? Does it give you the best mission return and financial return for the dollar, or are you just doing more of what you have always done? Social entrepreneurs constantly question whether their investment decisions are the best for the community, their constituency, and their mission. The question they ask is this: Is this a good investment in both mission and financial outcome? And, even though the answer is yes, they don't stop there. They ask a *second* question: Is there anywhere else we can get a better mission/money return?

❑ **For Example:** A symphony orchestra provided full orchestra concerts at a large regional concert hall, as well as smaller chamber orchestra concerts in a downtown church. The organization had been profitable for several years thanks to excellent fund-raising, good return season ticket sales, and an overwhelming response to the downtown venue for chamber orchestra concerts. The board wanted more linkage with the community, and it focused on the already-established programs with a number of local school districts. Students went to the large concert hall twice a year to hear a youth concert, with discussion before and after about the music.

The board talked with students, teachers, and school officials and found that there would be interest (and funds) from one of the school district foundations, as well as from the local arts council, if the symphony had small groups (quartet to octet size) come into each school and play for and then work with aspiring student musicians in a short workshop. The program was very mission-oriented and made a small profit. The board was pleased with the idea, but the staff noted that it was very time intense from the musicians' point of view and would preclude their full participation in another community linkage—free concerts of these same small groups in nursing homes throughout the community. The nursing home concert series had been a high mission priority for 10 years, one that was very well received.

What to do? By investing resources in the school, there was a mission and financial return. But those resources could not also be used in the nursing homes at the same time. This problem is what businesspeople call *opportunity cost,* the loss of the ability to use resources for one thing if you are using them for another. The board had to choose, and such a dilemma! Both programs were very deserving. What would your choice have been?

Next, a social entrepreneur knows the difference between needs and wants, and this is a very important realization. For some managers that I have talked to or worked with, it has been a true revelation. Here's the problem: Social entrepreneurs must be market-sensitive while still being mission-based. To do that, you have to regularly ask your markets (the people you serve, as well as the people who fund you) what they *want.* Now, most of us in the not-for-profit sector are driven by what people *need,* and we are very good at discerning that through observation, interview, testing, and the like. We do community *needs* assessments, talk constantly about meeting unmet *needs,* in short, we're *need* fillers. So, we focus on needs, not wants. The danger is that people seek what they want, not what they need. If we are to add value to our services, we must focus on wants and never assume we know what they are until we ask.

❏ **FOR EXAMPLE:** My favorite example of well-intentioned people giving people what they need, but not what they want is of a new director of a state child welfare system who, upon taking office, was justifiably appalled at the condition of the system as a whole and of the offices where the staff and clients interacted in particular. She sent teams of staff and consultants (including yours truly) to visit offices and to talk to staff and clients about ways to improve conditions rapidly. Most requests were pretty mundane and easy to fill: from the staff, we heard that they needed adequate supply of forms, phones that worked, heat that heated, clean rest rooms with toilet paper—that kind of thing. From clients in the waiting room, we heard the desire for less waiting time, a play area for the children, as well as the emphasis on rest rooms.

Our site visit team did many such visits in the first few months of the new director's tenure, but on the very first day, she accompanied us. As we walked into the huge client waiting room, the director's eye fell on the deli-like number sign on the wall at the end of the room. "NOW SERVING NUMBER 45" it said. The public address system weakly announced the same thing, crackling and spitting out the number of the next person to be served.

The director turned to me, a cold fury in her eyes. "We're fixing *that*," she fumed. "We are going to treat these people with respect and call them by name. This is awful." She was really mad about the numbers, and brought it up two or three times in the car on the way back to the central office. Later that day the memo went out to every office in the state: The number signs come down and we call people by name. A good, humane action. Or not.

Three weeks later I was in the same office, checking with the staff and clients whether they had received what they asked for—the forms, bathroom supplies, and so forth. Most of these things had been fixed, but when I went out into the waiting room to talk to the clients, I got a very different response than I expected. A huge man walked up to me, towering over me, and asked: "Are you the *fool* who took away the numbers on the wall?" I said I was just that person. Several other clients got up, walked over, and stood very, very close to me. One asked, "Why would you do something that *stupid?*" I replied (very, *very* politely) by asking them to explain to the fool why it was stupid. "Before, when we got our number, we knew how long we would have to wait. We could leave, go do something else, and come back. By taking away our numbers we're stuck here. We don't know how long it will be."

By giving the clients what they needed (in our eyes) we lowered the value of the service, imprisoning them at the office. Of course, the long-term solution was to reduce waiting times, but this one action, which was the only one we took that day without asking people if it was wanted, resulted in a *worse* perception of the organization. And a near heart attack for me.

Social entrepreneurs always seek ways to improve services, but by first asking the recipients of those services what they want.

Finally, social entrepreneurs always focus on mission outcomes. They remember that the first rule of not-for-profits is *"Mission, mission, and more mission!"* But they are more keenly aware than their nonentrepreneurial peers that the second rule is *"No money, no mission!"* and that it is a very close second. It is easy to get distracted from mission when you are taking risk, which is why we'll talk about staying focused in Chapter 12, "Final Thoughts."

So now we've set the stage by going over the characteristics of a social entrepreneur. Keep them in mind as we go through the rest of the book.

B. THE LINK BETWEEN SOCIAL ENTREPRENEURISM AND BUSINESS DEVELOPMENT

I've just told you that a key characteristic of a social entrepreneur is that of being willing to take reasonable risk on behalf of other people, the people your organization serves. Willingness to risk is inherent in the ability to innovate, grow, provide new and excellent services. But while I want you to take risks, I don't want you to take foolish risks, skydiving without a parachute. Enter the business planning or, as I will call it, the business development process. The entire idea of business development is to grow your mission capability with *reasonable* risk. We'll talk a lot more later about the adjective *reasonable,* but suffice it to say at this point that anyone who wants to be successful at social entrepreneurism needs to understand the business development process and its application to mission.

What do I mean when I use the term *business development?* Is it solely the issue of starting up a new business? What is the mission benefit in that? Does a new business or expansion of services have to be profitable? Does it have to be "housed" outside your existing corporate structure? The answers: no, I'll show you later, no, and no!

Later in this chapter, we'll go over the benefits of social entrepreneurship and business development and I'll show you many positive outcomes of using the business model for your mission-based business. You couldn't possibly garner all those benefits if they were only related to new products or services. Again, my hope for your organization is that you adopt the techniques of business development to assess the risks and benefits of a wide variety of new projects and activities. These would include (but not be limited to) the following.

1. The Starting of an Entirely New Product or Service

This is probably what most people think when they consider the term *business development:* something entirely new, and thus the most risky. Remember, all business, new or expanded, is risky. The idea of the business development process is to *reduce* your risk, but no business plan is ever risk-free.

❏ FOR EXAMPLE: The Litchfield Association for Retarded Citizens, in Torrington, Connecticut, started a gift and craft shop in late 1989. It continues today to operate profitably and contributes significant net income to the organization. A few of the items are crafts made by people with disabilities. Most are items made by area residents. The business gives the organization great visibility and credibility, and adds to its bottom line.

❏ FOR EXAMPLE: The Denver Children's Museum decided to take exhibits to where kids were—to shopping malls. They designed interactive exhibits that would attract their target market (children under 12) and then charged the malls a fee, since the malls in the Denver area are all competing with each other, and the museum was a real attraction for shoppers with children.

❏ FOR EXAMPLE: A school for behaviorally challenged adolescents in western Illinois was asked to present to a church Sunday school on the subject of "Dealing with Difficult Teenagers." The session was so successful that it decided to expand it to a three-hour workshop and take it on the road. The school rents meeting space in various communities, advertises the session, charges for admission—and nets nearly $65,000 per year.

❏ FOR EXAMPLE: An aquarium on the East Coast decided to investigate contract teaching in local school systems; a turnabout from having the kids come to the somewhat isolated location of the aquarium. Its business plan showed great promise, but cautioned it to invest in good classroom-teaching training for staff, and made it realize that it needed to add staff who specialized in going out into the community. The result? $15,000 income the first year, $45,000 the second (and a profit of $8,000), and much increased memberships and visitor counts directly tied to the children who were taught in the classroom.

Clearly, all of these organizations needed to go through the business development process. What they were attempting was new to them, and they realized that they did not know whether their ideas for service were even wanted in the community. Their success rested, in large part, on doing their homework before they went out and tried to start their businesses.

☞ **HANDS ON:** I also put fund-raising in this category, particularly if you have never done much of it before. Fund-raising needs to be looked at as a new business, not just something you go out and try. Is there a market? Do you have the core competencies to do the work well? Since you want your fund-raising to be a profit center (i.e., make money), do the numbers work? How soon will you get a return on your investment? Start thinking of all of your activities in this light.

2. A Major Expansion of an Existing Product or Service

Here, you have an opportunity to do more of something you already do. A piece of cake, right? Not necessarily. Expanding takes up an enormous amount of time, energy, and here is the most important thing people forget, *cash.* All the same questions that are asked in a new start-up hold true in an expansion: Is there demand for what I want to do? Is there enough demand to justify my investment? Am I getting enough mission for my organization's money? Look at it this way: You may have gone through a period where you, to steal from the movie *Field of Dreams,* "built it and they came." But just because they did, does not necessarily mean that if you build more of it, more of them will show up.

❑ **FOR EXAMPLE:** Your organization is presented with a funding opportunity from your key government funder, or a local foundation, or United Way. It requires you to increase the volume of an existing service by 40 percent over the next two years. Should you? Most readers would answer almost immediately: "If they'll pay, we'll do it." Wrong answer. An expansion of this size is incredibly taxing on the organization. Look before you leap. Is there enough payment up front to allow you to afford the expansion? What will be the impact on your administrative, human resource, transportation, and computer systems? How about staff? Can you find adequate people to do this added work? Does the expansion align with your strategic plan? Is what the funder wants to pay for really wanted in the community? How will you pay for this service when and if the funding ends?

These, and hundreds of other questions need to be answered before you leap into an expanded service project. The business development process will help you to see what you are jumping into clearly and before you jump.

❑ **FOR EXAMPLE:** Let's look at the issue laid out in the previous example with some actual numbers. Imagine this scenario:

1. Your major funder gives you notice that it is awarding you a *$1 million* contract for *one year* starting the first of next month!

2. The contract is *full-cost reimbursable,* and it is in an area where you have expertise, can find the staff, and get going on schedule. The funder pays you in 45 days and will pay all costs up to $1 million!

3. There are *no costs* incurred before the start of the project!

4. The service is a *high-mission priority* for you!

Is this a good deal? For the mission—*absolutely!* For the organization? Let's see. . . . How much does this no-risk, full-reimbursement contract really cost?

If you bill the funder after the first 30 days of the contract, and it actually pays in exactly 45 days, what has happened? You have *loaned the funder $205,479 interest-free* for the remainder of the contract. Don't believe me? Just divide $1 million by 365 days to get the per day cost. Then multiply that by the 75 days it takes to get your first payment.

Here's the lesson: *If you don't have $205,000 to invest, you can't afford the "no-risk" $1 million!*

Of course, in most cases it would be much worse than this, as you would have large start-up costs. I've given this example in hundreds of training sessions over the years, and people are always coming up to me afterward saying, "So *that's* why we're always broke! We break even on every contract, but we're getting deeper and deeper in the hole!"

Will business planning change the funder's mind on its speed of payment? Probably not. But it will give you the knowledge to make good business decisions, and not get yourself in a cash hole you can't dig yourself out of.

3. The Expansion of an Existing Activity for a New Group of People

This would mean working for a new demographic group, or it could mean working for people who can (or cannot) pay directly for services. You would be assuming that you could do what you do well now for a group of people (a market) who might have very different wants.

❑ **FOR EXAMPLE:** In the mid-1980s I worked with a large number of alcohol and drug rehabilitation centers. Most of these facilities were state funded and most had a heavy percentage of clients who had, at one point or another, wound up living on the street or in prison, or both. The staff were dedicated, well-trained, and, to the level you can be with any addiction, successful. The executive directors and boards of these organizations wanted to move away from their dependence on state funding, and thus had decided to seek clients from the corporate sector, clients who would be reimbursable by traditional insurance and their employers' Employee Assistance Programs. Their assumption was that, since the per day fee for insurance-covered clients was $40 more, they would make a ton of money.

To understate the case, these organizations weren't ready. No corporate executive would set foot in most of these facilities. In addition, most of the operations were not ready to be certified by the insurer. No one had seriously considered the cost of getting ready to provide service for this new category of clients. They assumed that a few brochures, a couple of phone calls, and some staff training and they would be ready to go. No way.

The business development process helps you find out in advance what your markets want and whether your core competencies match up with those wants. This can help you avoid costly moves into areas that you are not yet ready to serve, and can assure that you focus on what you do *well,* not just what you do.

4. The Expansion of an Existing Activity into a New Geographic Area

The most common example of this is a not-for-profit that decides to start providing services in another township, city, county, or state. Sometimes, such a move is part of an overall strategic plan of growth. More commonly, though, a not-for-profit chases available dollars from a government or foundation funder who has identified an unfilled need and issued a Request for Proposal (RFP) to seek service providers.

A couple of key points here. First, even if you have been successful in community A, that does not insure that you will be successful in communities B, C, or D. The for-profit and not-for-profit worlds are both full of stories of organizations that were on the A-list in their home communities, but couldn't make it in a different locale. There is a great line in the first scene of the Broadway musical "The Music Man," in which a character states to another aspiring traveling salesman, "You gotta know the territory!" Very true, and the business planning process helps you find out what local issues such as culture, language, and acceptance of your service model will affect your expansion. Second, more and more RFPs are being opened up to for-profits or to the best not-for-profits from across your state or region. As a result, you are in a much more competitive environment. If you don't go through the business planning process, you are going to be less competitive. Because I guarantee your competition is doing their homework.

5. The Purchase of an Existing Business

In this situation, your organization might be interested in purchasing a business to further your mission, rather than starting one from scratch. With your purchase, you buy customers, salespeople, and, we hope, some goodwill. This is not as unusual as you might think.

❏ **FOR EXAMPLE:** An animal shelter wanted to expand its service and revenue base and was considering starting up a service that provided the community with pet care services in people's homes while they were away on business or vacation. In researching their business plan, the animal shelter identified three competitors. One of the competition (the largest) heard about their inquiries, came to them, and offered to sell. It turned out that while the owner *loved* animals, she had discovered that she *hated* running a business. The shelter ran through the planning process and worked out a way to buy the business over four years, while keeping the former owner on as a shelter manager.

Buying a business is a different approach, and one that is often cash heavy early on in the process. There are many, many things to consider, and going through the planning process helps you think them through and reduce your risk.

6. The Merger or Partnership with an Existing Organization

Mergers, collaborations, and partnerships are an ever increasing part of the not-for-profit culture. As funders focus more on outcomes and encourage competition, the pace of "getting larger" is rapidly increasing. For you, this means that you may have to consider an offer to merge or collaborate, or you may decide to make such an offer to another organization. The business-planning process will help you consider your options, the good and bad that could come from such an effort, and, again, help reduce your risk.

❏ **FOR EXAMPLE:** The Hope Network in Grand Rapids, Michigan, has made a strategy of growth through merger, acquisition, partnership, and providing management services. It started out with the idea of trying to grow only through merger, but as it proceeded through its planning efforts, it discovered that not-for-profits wanted a wide array of affiliation choices. Hope provided those, and, as of this writing, was affiliated in some manner with over 40 other not-for-profits, to the mission benefit of all of them, through a variety of economies of scale.

Hope could not have succeeded if it had just followed its initial instincts. It needed to carefully gauge the market before it started, and then be flexible during the business start-up.

All of these are real-world applications of the business development model, situations that your organization may have already faced, or that will be under consideration in the next few months or year. I hope you see that by using an organized, systematic, businesslike process, you can do more than just start a new business, you can rework your entire way of looking at your mission.

C. THE USES OF SOCIAL ENTREPRENEURISM TO DO MORE MISSION

I wouldn't be surprised if there are still people in your organization who don't like the idea of thinking in business terms, who suspect anything labeled as "business," and who consider use of such a term counterproductive, even traitorous. To help you change their minds, let's look at some examples of how this process can help your organization do more mission.

1. *More direct mission.* The vast majority (95 percent) of the organizations that I have helped develop business plans for new businesses have developed businesses that provided direct services. Why? Because the provision of service is what they know. Look at the previous example about the aquarium. It had new revenue streams but was providing a direct educational service. The same is true with the school that provided training to parents. A business? Yes. A service? Absolutely, and one that no outside funder would fund. Here's the key: The business *expanded the organization's mission impact.*

2. *More money for more mission.* As you look at different business opportunities, you will find things that make money, and things that don't. Earlier I noted that fund-raising should be looked at as a new business. You certainly want it to make money! But there will also be services that are potentially profitable. Those profits, if realized, can support other services that, while being crucial mission, are not paying completely for themselves. Thus, businesses can spin off funds for more mission elsewhere.

   I need to emphasize here that I have absolutely no problem with any of your programs losing money (being a loss center, in business terms). If you have a mission need in your community, and you feel the mission outcome is worth the financial cost, good for you. Just make sure that your organization as a whole is not a loss center! And, this is where developing a new, profitable business can help: The profits can go directly to subsidize the high-mission loss center.

3. *Doing the mission that you do really well.* No business succeeds, or even survives for long, without providing quality services. In later chapters, we'll discuss core competence at length, but now I want to make the point that, if you apply the business-planning model to your operations, you will see that quality and competence are crucial to your long-term success. I have seen organization after organization ramp up their training on quality as a direct result of looking at their competition more closely, as well as listening to their markets about what is important to those markets.

4. *No longer doing what people don't want.* This part is painful in the short run, and really beneficial in the long run. As you begin to use the business development model throughout your organization, you will almost certainly find that you are doing things that people no longer really want, or in a way that is no longer satisfactory. If you listen to your markets and your research, you will then make the decision to focus on what you can do well (your competencies) that matches up with what your customers want. I'm not going to try to tell you that this is easy; it's not. But it allows you to focus, a crucial skill of a successful mission-based manager. And, in focusing, you can get the most mission possible from your available resources.

D. THE BENEFITS TO THE ORGANIZATION

We've established that your mission will benefit from adapting to the social entrepreneurism model. How about your organization? Here are some direct benefits to consider.

1. *More income and long-term stability.* Applying the social entrepreneurial model results in more income and better long-term stability in *most* not-for-profits. Why? Because it helps the organization develop new methods of service delivery and/or income. It is more likely to result in net income in new programs. And, it helps the organization make better financial and mission choices about expansion efforts. Why doesn't it help *every* not-for-profit make more money? Because, whether you are a for-profit or a not-for-profit, business is risky. As I said earlier, the idea of the business development process is to help *reduce* your risk, not to eliminate it. No plan, no matter how well researched, how brilliantly conceived, guarantees business success. That having been said, your business decisions will be more informed and more likely to succeed using this model, and you will begin to seek income from places you never have previously.

2. *A focus on core competence and customer satisfaction.* As you begin to apply your business development knowledge to the tasks facing you, you will quickly realize that competence and quality of service are crucial, and that no one cares any more that you are a not-for-profit when they gauge that quality and competence. Hopefully, this enlightenment will spread throughout the organization and help you improve the quality of everything you do. I know from experience that business development training turns people who are ambivalent about investing in quality into true believers in such investments. This focus on quality has a corollary: the realization that the organization must set its sights on constant customer satisfaction, not just customer service. We'll talk about this more at length when we get into marketing issues. But, the key point here is that organizations that are concerned about satisfaction are concerned about whether the customer got what he or she *wanted, from the customer's point of view.* Organizations that focus on customer service are focused on what the customer *needed, from the service provider's point of view.*

❑ **FOR EXAMPLE:** You order a pizza delivered to your home from a pizza restaurant who promises delivery in 40 minutes from the time of your call. The pizza comes in 35 minutes. The pizza parlor has just met one of its quality standards which states: "Deliver every pizza in the time promised when the order is placed." But you'll never order from them again. Why? Because the pizza was cold. The delivery person left the insulating bag open while driving to your home and also had the window open to vent cigarette smoke. Thus, the cold pizza. See the difference. The restaurant measured only what *it* thought was important: speed. *You* were concerned about having edible pizza. Would you have been happy if it had been hot, but not delivered for an hour? Probably not. But a customer satisfaction checklist would include a number of things (on time, hot, polite delivery, etc.) that came from some research into customer wants.

In businesslike not-for-profit organizations, the idea of customer satisfaction is paramount. It should be for your organization as well.

3. *Better knowledge of who you* really *work for.* By looking at the organizations and people that interact with your organization, you will discover that you actually work for a bunch more folks than you had previously thought. Social entrepreneurism requires that you look at the people you serve, the people who are employed by you, the people that volunteer for you, and the people that pay you all as equal

markets, whose wants are to be investigated and met to the utmost degree possible. Put more simply, if you think that your only customer is a person who receives service from you, think again. The knowledge of your entire customer base is often a revelation to the management team and board, and begins the process of understanding why there is so much conflict about resource allocation within an organization that was previously thought to be focused only on its service recipients. And understanding that conflict can help you solve a great deal of it.

E. THE RISKS OF NOT USING THE MODEL

Now that I've told you all the good that can come from applying the social entrepreneurial model regularly in your decision making, let's look at what happens if you decide not to.

1. You Just Chase Dollars

Way too many not-for-profits chase dollars rather than invest resources. I know that this sounds patronizing, but it is true. Let's look at a very common example of a human service provider's organizational chart, seen in Exhibit 2-1.

As you can see, this organization started out in 1977 as a counseling center for chronically mentally ill individuals. Through the years, it has added job placement services for its clients, residential services (group homes) as state institutions were closed, community housing financed through the Department of Housing and Urban Development (HUD), a day care service for critically mentally ill individuals, some recreation services and later a camp, transportation services to move everyone from service to service, and, most recently, welfare to work services. I regularly see organizational charts like this, as have you, I suspect. The expansion progression is pretty common for our not-for-profit world. But let's look at it another way. This agency is in eight completely different businesses: counseling, day care, a hotel, a landlord, a bus company, an employment agency, welfare reform, and a camp. Do you see any relationship in these businesses apart from the client being mentally ill? I don't.

The question I always ask the staff and board of such agencies is, "How did you get from where you started to where you are now? When you started a day care, or acquired the camp, did you have staff who were good at it? Did you do a feasibility study? Did you study the industry?" Their answer? *"No, we got a grant."*

Exhibit 2-1   Model organization chart.

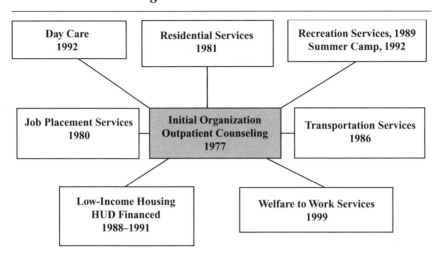

They got a grant. They chased the money. And they got away with it because the not-for-profit world was not the competitive marketplace that it is today. Using the business model and becoming smart social entrepreneurs will keep you from just chasing the money, *and just chasing the money is something you can no longer afford to do.* If you don't use the business development model, you will be doomed to continue to just chase dollars endlessly, whether you can do the service that the money pays for well or not. And, in this environment, that will be fatal.

2. You Make Poorer Resource Investment Decisions

You are, as a staff person or volunteer of a not-for-profit, a steward of the resources you have at your command. Good stewards make optimal use of those resources to further their organization's mission to the benefit of the community. That means weighing the costs of the investment and the benefits that may accrue from it. If you use all your staff on one type of service, you can't simultaneously provide any other type of service. If you spend all your money on a building, you don't have any funds to pay staff. If you decide to hire a fund-raiser, you have to pay his or her costs for a year or two until the fund-raiser begins to be a profit center. During that time, that money can't be used for anything else. You may not have realized it, but all your resource allocation decisions are investment decisions, and the business-planning model is a terrific tool to help you make better investments of the resources you have. If you don't take the time to use the concepts in business planning, you won't have the tools to be able to make the best decision. And, again, you won't be doing your job as well as you could.

3. You Don't Keep Up with the Changing Needs of Your Markets

Successful businesses and competent social entrepreneurs know that the markets in which they operate are constantly changing. Thus, they operate with the assumption that things will change, and so will they. They use the tools of social entrepreneuring (market assessments, innovation, risk) to stay as close to their markets as possible. Organizations that don't act in a businesslike manner just stay on course, doing the same-old same-old, and get left behind by their competition.

❏ **FOR EXAMPLE:** In the 1980s even though the computer world was rapidly moving to a desktop platform, IBM, who legitimized the PC, kept spending most of its R&D (research and development) money and nearly all of its marketing dollars on mainframes, which fewer and fewer businesses purchased. As a result, IBM lost money for the first time ever, was threatened by outside competition in the form of Compaq and Dell, and nearly was forced out of a crucial market, until it started to pay attention to its markets.

You need to ask, listen, innovate, and respond to your markets, and the social entrepreneur model shows you how to do that.

4. You Are Less Competitive

As a result of all of these factors, your organization is less competitive than it could be. Less competitive for funds, for staff, for good board members, for donors, and, of course, for people to serve. And, whether you like it or not, whether you agree with the changes in policy or rue the day they were envisioned, the world in which you work has irrevocably become more competitive. Not-for-profits must adapt to this environment, or they will cease to exist.

5. You Are Less Mission-Capable

This, of course, is ultimately the bottom line. If you don't apply the social entrepreneur model to your resource investment decisions, you aren't as mission-capable as you would be if you did use the model to get the most mission for your money. There is no way for me to mince words: It's bad stewardship. This method of making business decisions, this sequence of activities that allows you to seek new ways to serve the community, this tried and true decision algorithm, works. It works for for-profits. It works for not-for-profits. It can make your organization better, more responsive, more financially stable, more focused, more mission-capable.

I hope that I have talked you into the idea that business development and social entrepreneurism are good things for you, for your organization, and for your community. In Chapter 3, The Business Development Process, we'll walk through the process step by step.

RECAP

In this chapter, we covered some important ground that needed to be discussed before you learn the process of business development and social entrepreneuring. First, we defined the characteristics of the social entrepreneur. To reinforce these important traits, let's review them again. They are as follows:

Social entrepreneurs are constantly looking for new ways to serve their constituencies and to add value to existing services.

They are willing to take reasonable risk on behalf of the people that their organization serves.

They understand the difference between needs and wants.

They understand that all resource allocations are really stewardship investments.

They weigh the social and financial return of each of these investments.

They always keep mission first, but know that without money, there is no mission output.

I made the point that social entrepreneurs are mission-driven, but look at their organizations' work, and their work within the organization as one of never resting and always pushing forward to do more mission and better mission, to be flexible, innovative, and responsive.

Next, we identified what I am going to use as the definition of the term *business development.* It was defined as one or more of the following applications:

1. The starting of an *entirely new* product or service
2. A major expansion of an existing product or service
3. The expansion of an existing activity for *a new group of people*
4. The expansion of an existing activity into *a new geographic area*
5. The *purchase* of an existing business
6. The *merger or partnership* with an existing organization

Third, we looked at what the benefits of applying the whole idea of business development are to the end recipients—your clientele. We asked the question, what are the benefits to the organization in terms of direct mission? The answers were as follows:

1. More direct mission
2. More money for more mission
3. Doing the mission that you do really well
4. No longer doing what people don't want

Fourth, we examined the benefits of the model to the organization as a whole. These included the following three important outcomes:

1. More income and long-term stability
2. A focus on core competence and customer satisfaction
3. Better knowledge of who you work for

Finally, we examined what happens if you stick to the old ways of not looking at decisions as investments of resources.

1. You just chase dollars.
2. You make poorer resource investment decisions.
3. You don't keep up with the changing needs of your markets.
4. You are less competitive.
5. You are less mission-capable.

If you started this chapter as a skeptic, I hope that there is no longer any doubt in your mind that good mission equals good business, and good business can equate to more mission, sooner, in a higher-quality manner. I hope you now know that business development and social entrepreneurism have a wide variety of applications to your mission. I hope I showed you enough mission-based benefits that you will be able to convince your staff and board that working in this manner is worth the time and effort needed to make the change.

But don't decide until you actually see the model and how it has worked for many, many of your not-for-profit peers. That's the subject of our next chapter.

QUESTIONS FOR DISCUSSION: CHAPTER 2

1. How do we measure up to Peter's list of the characteristics of a social entrepreneur? Where are we strong? Where can we improve?

2. Do we chase the dollars or really pursue our mission? How can we be better at investing our resources? Do we look at our expenditures as investments?

3. What are our core competencies? Do we have any that are more important than others? How can we improve them?

4. Are we pushing for customer service or customer satisfaction? Do we understand the difference? Is it an important one?

5. Are we competitive now, and how can/should we view competition in our field and in our community?

3

The Business
Development Process

OVERVIEW

In this chapter you will learn about the following:

➤ The Seven Steps of the Not-for-Profit Business Development
Process
➤ A Social Entrepreneurship Readiness Assessment Tool

Social entrepreneurship doesn't just happen. It takes some long-term
changes in attitude, willingness to take risk, perspective, and finance. At its
core, social entrepreneurism is an idea that taking risk on behalf of the
people you serve is a good thing, not something to be avoided at all costs.
But more than that, social entrepreneurs make use of established business
development practices to keep that risk reasonable.

Business development is not new and certainly no longer particularly
innovative for not-for-profits in general. There are thousands of your peers
who have developed successful businesses to further their mission. But
what is special is *your* business, your organization, and in this chapter
we'll provide you with two key steps in the journey to becoming a social
entrepreneur. First, we'll look at the steps of the business development
process. We'll look at these in detail, and then move to a tool that will help
you gauge whether you are ready to proceed or need some more prepara-
tion before you embark on your trip to entrepreneurism.

A. THE SEVEN STEPS OF THE NOT-FOR-PROFIT BUSINESS
DEVELOPMENT PROCESS

There is a sequence of steps to follow, a process that works for not-for-
profits that develop new businesses, expand existing ones, or acquire outside ventures. This process is significantly different in its initial stages

than that of a for-profit organization. Thus, you cannot just adapt a for-profit business model for your organization. As I said in Chapter 2, The Benefits of the Social Entrepreneurism Model, you are a *mission-based* business, not a for-profit one. You need to use the *mission-based* process that we'll discuss in the following pages. If you do, you'll be much more likely to succeed.

In Chapter 2, you read about the many applications that this model has for your not-for-profit. We also discussed how social entrepreneurs use the business development model to weigh their investment decisions and to decide on new services and expansions. Remember, the process can be adapted to any of the various applications we discussed in Chapter 2. In other words, it works just as well for evaluating the risks of a new service as it does for the expansion of an existing one. The seven steps are as follows:

1. Review your mission.
2. Establish the risk willingness of your organization.
3. Establish the mission outcomes of the business.
4. Idea generation.
5. Feasibility studies (preliminary and final).
6. Business plan (including the financials).
7. Implementation plan with accountability.

Now let's look at each in detail.

1. Review Your Mission

Everything in a not-for-profit starts and ends with mission. It's the reason you exist, and it is your ultimate product. And, in the business development process, it's the first step. You need to sit down with your staff and board members and talk through your mission statement. Why? First, because it's always good to regularly review not only what your mission says (the actual words) but, more importantly, what it *means (what the outcomes of the words are)*. You will find (as I always do) that, while your staff and board may well know the words of the mission, they are not unanimous in their interpretation of the outcomes. This is important to know now, because it affects their outlook on risk (which we'll get to in a minute) and on resource allocation. If, for example, your board feels that your focus should be on improving quality of service (doing the *best* possible service) while the staff feels that it should be on expansion (doing the *most* possible service), there will be a conflict. So, have this discussion first.

Then, talk through whether your business expansion, new business, or merger is appropriate given the culture of your organization, the political situation in your community, and the status of your internal financial and staff capacity. The key question here is, is this business idea the best use of your limited resources *now?* You want to garner input and then, hopefully, consensus, that pursuing this idea through the feasibility and business plan stages makes sense at this time. It may well be a great idea to expand, to merge, or to start a new service. But it also may well be that it is *not* a good idea today, this week, or even this fiscal year. Talk it through in a mission context.

☞ **HANDS ON:** Now is a great time to organize a social entrepreneurism team in your organization. Like all internal committees, I recommend that you include staff from all levels of the organization, top to bottom, a volunteer or two, and some skilled outsiders if possible. Examples of skilled outsiders could be people with financial, business development, or marketing expertise. You get a much better set of perspectives with such a group, and the staff development that accrues is terrific. Your team should review the mission, and then be responsible for the risk assessment that we'll discuss in the next section. They can be the focal point of all your business development activities, become the most familiar (and comfortable) with the business development process, and eventually train other staff in its application.

Pick this group carefully. You don't want all "yes" people in the group, and you do need to include people from management, from finance, and from service provision. Others can be brought in for expertise on particular business ideas. For example, if implementation of a certain business would require transportation, you can bring in a staff person who is responsible for that area to consult, but not all of your ideas will require transportation. Get people who are eager to learn, who are committed to your mission, and who are willing to try new things on your team.

2. Establish the Risk Willingness of Your Organization

We all have a different willingness to take risks. Some of us seem to thrive on risk, some avoid it *at all costs.* This is true physically (people who love mountain climbing, hang gliding, or other pasttimes perceived as high-risk) as well as financially (people who invest in commodity options, penny stocks, and other high-risk financial instruments). The interesting thing about this is, of course, that what is seen as unacceptably risky to one person is seen as totally acceptable to another. And the risk-taking appetite changes within the individual as conditions change.

❏ **FOR EXAMPLE:** I am a private pilot and fly a four-seat, one-engine plane. Many people consider that reckless, while I find it a manageable risk. On the other hand, I would never, ever get on a motorcycle, having worked in an emergency room for four years in college. And, I have a son who loves to snowboard and in-line skate, neither of which I will try now, but both of which I would have embraced as a (more flexible and athletic) teen.

As I noted earlier, the not-for-profit community in general has been historically much too risk-averse, preferring to do more of the same rather than to try something new, something that might fail. We'll talk more about the cultural and financial reasons for this risk aversion in the next chapter, but for the moment let's focus on the fact that all activities, whether brand new, or just expansions, or even doing the same old thing, entail some risk, and thus your organization must establish its risk comfort zone.

All business is risky. The better the business idea, the more skilled the providers, the more honed the business plan, the *lower* the risk, but risk never disappears completely from the equation. The question you, your staff, and board need to tackle at this stage of the process is this: How much risk are we comfortable with? What you don't want to have happen is for the staff to jump into a new business effort, feeling that the investment of time and money is a good one, and have the board, the community, or a key funder feel that such a resource allocation is totally inappropriate for you.

Talk through the fact that all business is risky and what the various risks are that the business entails: money, staff and volunteer time, and political capital in your community. On the other hand, there is also the risk of inaction, of being passed up by competitors, of losing a potentially important market. Find out where the organization is in terms of risk, and find out *before* you actually start planning the business. I'll give you a lot more guidance in this area in Chapter 4, First Steps: Mission Outcomes, Risk, and Idea Generation.

3. Establish the Mission Outcomes of the Business

Here is, perhaps, the most important step in the not-for-profit business development process. You need to decide on, and then widely disseminate, the mission outcomes you intend to generate from your business. For example, if your new business is a day care center for Alzheimer's patients, the mission outcome would be the day care for a certain number of people. If that center was also budgeted to make money, the mission outcome would also be what those profits would be used for. While not all of the profits would go directly to some other program (as some would probably be retained to help the day care center grow), some could be targeted, and I recommend that the use be as personal and as mission-oriented as possible. Don't tell people that the profits are going to repair the roof, repave the parking lot, or some other *necessary*, but not particularly *motivating*, task.

Why? Because the idea of this step in the planning process is just that: motivation. All of your staff, I am sure, have full days and probably feel that they have 2.75 full-time-equivalents (FTE) living in their bodies. What you are going to do now is to ask them to work harder. And, if this is your first foray into an outside business, merger, or expansion, you'll find that there is resistance to the idea on its merits. ("Why are we trying to set up a new business or expand when there is so much still to do with what we are already engaged in?") Thus, having specific, personal, mission-based outcomes for the business laid out at this stage in the process has three effects. First, it motivates staff, who now see a valid reason for their additional efforts. Second, it sets the bar fairly high for the social entrepreneur team, assuring that they will be concerned with mission outcomes, and not just financial return. Third, it reminds everyone of the point of the exercise: more mission capability for the organization. Don't skip this step. It is a crucial bridge that allows many staff and volunteers to follow you on the journey to entrepreneurism. Again, we'll talk more about this important step in Chapter 4, First Steps: Mission Outcomes, Risk, and Idea Generation.

4. Idea Generation

After completing the first three steps, you are finally ready to seriously look at different ideas of what your business should do. Should you provide a new service, expand or improve an existing one, move into a new territory, or even acquire a competitor? Perhaps you started the process "knowing" what you are going to do. If so, think again. You don't *know* anything yet. You have ideas, suspicions, gut feelings, and instincts about what will work, but you don't know whether an idea will work until you go through the remainder of the process.

And here is the other key point: There may be a better idea than yours out there, and now is the time to find out. At this stage you open up the floor to everyone involved in your organization, asking for their ideas on what you can do to serve the community and make money doing it. This broadens the number of ideas to consider and involves staff early in the process. Remember, most of your staff are much closer to the line of service than you are. They see the needs every day and know the capacity of themselves and their fellow workers to add more onto their plates. Get their ideas, input, and involvement early on. In Chapter 4, First Steps: Mission Outcomes, Risk, and Idea Generation, we'll talk at length about how to work with your staff to generate ideas and how to sort those ideas carefully to find the ones that best suit your situation.

5. Feasibility Studies (Preliminary and Final)

Once you have identified a set of business possibilities, it is time to find out if they are the right ideas at the right time for your organization. You will do this by running the ideas through a preliminary and then a final feasibility study. In the preliminary study, you'll delineate the core service of your business and your target market(s) and examine the industry that you will be operating in. This quick analysis will tell you whether it makes sense to spend more time in researching and writing your final feasibility study. Since you will have generated a large number of business ideas, you will have the ability to run the two or three best of these through the preliminary feasibility study and take the best of these on to the final study.

In your final feasibility study, you will do a lot more research and writing. You will ask and answer dozens of crucial questions about the business idea. At the end of this work, you will have a pretty good idea of whether the business is feasible at this time for your organization.

Feasibility studies help reduce the risk of business development by letting you really examine the idea in detail, asking the question, "Can we do this business well?" Once you have finished this study, you will have done a great amount of the work necessary to complete your business plan. In Chapter 5, Feasibility Studies, we'll cover feasibility studies in great detail.

6. Business Plan (Including the Financials)

Now is the time (finally!) to write the business plan itself. By this point, you have thought through your willingness to take risk, decided on mission goals for the business, generated a list of ideas, narrowed them down, run the best of the ideas through the preliminary and final feasibility study grinder, and now you are ready to take the best and put it into the language of business: the business plan. This is an important step and, oddly enough, one that many not-for-profits skip, feeling that they have done enough work already, and "time's a-wastin'." Don't repeat their mistake. You need a business plan.

❏ **FOR EXAMPLE:** If I am on your board and you come to me and say, "I need $145,000 to double the size of our day care center," my answer will be, "Show me your business plan." If I am a banker and you come to me and say, "I need a $70,000 loan to finance the expansion of our wonderful day care center," my answer will be, "Show me your business plan." And, if I am a vendor of day care supplies such as diapers, formula, and toys, and you come to me and say, "We're going to double our day care size in a year. We'll be doubling our orders from you, but I need you to let us pay in 60 days rather than 30 for the first year," I'll answer—you guessed it—"Show me your business plan."

You need a business plan that focuses you and the reader on your core product or service, the target markets you have identified, how you are going to compete, your marketing plan, what things can go wrong (and your plans to deal with them), and how you are going to pay for everything. And, I'll show you how to do this in Chapter 6, The Business Plan, where we'll walk through the development of a full business plan, and then in Chapter 7, Business Plan Financial Projections, where I'll show you how to develop the financials that go with the plan.

7. Implementation Plan with Accountability

Now that the plan is done, you need to first get it approved, and then put it into action. This seemingly simple part of the process is actually fraught with all kinds of problems, delays, and frustrations. You may have to deal with bankers; you may well have to interact with regulators; you need to be accountable to your staff, your board, and your community. And, of course, the rest of your organization continues apace as well. So how do you do that?

You use the plan as guidance. As you implement, your plan's goals and objectives will help you keep on task and on schedule. The budgets and cash flow projections will keep you in line financially. And, when the situation changes, you can use your overall mission goals to help you make sure you keep focused on the most important part of social entrepreneurship: mission enhancement.

Speaking of changing conditions: They will. Don't let your plan lock you in to actions that are counterproductive. If the situation changes, change your plan, or stop the implementation of the business. The entire idea of business planning is to reduce your risks. The business plan that you have worked so hard to develop discusses the worth of a certain business within a certain set of business conditions. If those conditions have changed, the value of the business as an investment has changed as well, perhaps for the better, perhaps for worse.

❏ **FOR EXAMPLE:** I work with lots of organizations that have recycling businesses. Recycling is a terrific idea, but only when the commodity price (the price the business can get for recycled aluminum, glass, plastic, or paper) is reasonable. You can write a terrific business plan for recycling this week that is torpedoed by a drop in commodity prices next week. When that happens, these organizations rethink their business conditions, their prices, and the return on investment quickly. If they didn't, they could be chasing a good business idea down a price decline into a bottomless pit.

Now the accountability part. What this means is that you are accountable to the policies set by the board, the strategy set by your social entrepreneur team, and the goals and objectives in the plan. Make sure that you review where you are in the plan every two or three days at first, then weekly, then every two weeks, but never less frequently than once a month. This will help assure that you both stay on track and that you are aware of any changing conditions that merit alterations in your plans.

Again, the seven steps in the not-for-profit business development cycle are as follows:

1. Review your mission.
2. Establish the risk willingness of your organization.
3. Establish the mission outcomes of the business.
4. Idea generation.
5. Feasibility studies (preliminary and final).
6. Business plan (including the financials).
7. Implementation plan with accountability.

While most businesspeople in the for-profit sector would skip the first three steps, as a not-for-profit manager, you cannot afford to. You need to pay attention to your mission, your organization's willingness to take risk, and how the venture will support your mission before you proceed through the idea, feasibility, and business plan stages. If you don't, you will either founder or you will need to return and do these steps later, when it will be more time-consuming and more confusing to your staff and board. Do them in order.

Now that you know the process in brief, are you ready to proceed? Let's find out.

B. A SOCIAL ENTREPRENEURSHIP READINESS ASSESSMENT TOOL

Are you ready to be a social entrepreneur? Do your staff, your board, and your volunteers have what it takes to take risk on behalf of the people you serve? Is your organization set up for the added stress and strain? Are your systems in place? Is the expertise available? All good questions, and all ones that you want to answer as soon as possible.

Many, many not-for-profits dive into their social entrepreneurial process before they are ready to start. I am sure that right about now you are chomping at the bit to get underway. You probably have a great idea, you may feel that you have the board and staff ready to go and, most importantly, you have people in need in your community. So why wait? Because, if you are not really ready, you almost certainly doom yourself to failure. So, take a deep breath and have your SE team answer the questions in Exhibit 3-1.

☞ **HANDS ON:** Have the entire group answer the questions, not just one or two individuals. If you just do this yourself, it is much harder to be truly objective. A group is much more likely to be. Copy the following pages, and have each member of your team fill them out alone. Then come back together and compare your answers. You'll wind up with the collective wisdom of the members of the group regarding this important self-assessment.

There are 24 items to review in the list in Exhibit 3-1. If more than eight answers are "No," I'd go back and take the time to improve your score. You need to have your organization in good shape to move ahead before you develop a new, and inevitably risky, venture.

RECAP

In this chapter, we've taken a look at the core of social entrepreneurism. We have reviewed for the first time the seven steps of the not-for-profit business development process, discussed each briefly, and noted how important it is to do the steps in order. The seven steps of the process are as follows:

1. Review your mission.
2. Establish the risk willingness of your organization.
3. Establish the mission outcomes of the business.
4. Idea generation.
5. Feasibility studies (preliminary and final).
6. Business plan (including the financials).
7. Implementation plan with accountability.

Exhibit 3-1   Social Entrepreneurship Readiness checklist.

Area	Readiness Item	Yes	No	Don't know
Mission				
	Have the staff and board reviewed the idea of business development in relation to the organization's mission statement?			
	Are revisions or updates of the mission necessary?			
	Have you decided on the mission uses for the business and the mission uses for any profits?			
Risk				
	Have the board and staff discussed the risk inherent in new business development?			
	Have limits been set on venture capital to put at risk?			
	Do your board and staff view resource allocations as investments rather than expenditures?			
	Do your board and staff understand that the desired outcome for a not-for-profit business is a mix of mission return and financial return?			
Systems				
	Does the organization have personnel and finance policies that have been revised in the past 24 months?			
	Does the organization have a strategic plan that is current?			
	Does the organization have the information systems, payroll, accounts payable, and receivable systems that can accommodate growth?			
	Is the organization's financial accounting software able to track multiple projects and/or businesses?			
Skills				
	Are all of the following skills available within the staff and governing volunteers: planning, budgeting, pricing, marketing, project management?			
	Are skills and experience available within the industry or area that you have chosen to pursue?			
	Has the management team made the commitment to allow talented and experienced individuals to use their skills to develop the new business?			
	Have you generated a list of your organization's core competencies?			
Space				
	Is there readily available appropriate physical space to house the business?			
	Is there adequate equipment, wiring, plumbing, ventilation, security, and lighting for the business?			
Finance				
	Has the organization as a whole been profitable the past three years?			
	Does the organization have at least 90 days of cash or cash equivalents on hand?			
	Does the organization have an excellent relationship with its banker?			
	Does the organization have a line of credit?			
	Does the organization have a current ratio of 1.0 or higher?			
	Does the organization have a debt to net worth of 0.3 or less?			
	Will any of your funders penalize you for any net income from the business?			
TOTALS:	Add up the number of yes, no, and don't know answers and put the totals in the column to the right.			

After this review, I provided you the opportunity to see where your organization stands in terms of readiness for social entrepreneurial activity. You should have filled in Exhibit 3-1 which allowed you to come up with a preliminary score on your entrepreneurial readiness.

So now that you know how ready you are and what is ahead, it is time to get to specifics. The next four chapters will give you the information to go through the process efficiently and profitably. In the next chapter, we'll cover mission, risk, and idea generation in detail. Chapter 5 will look at feasibility studies, Chapter 6, the business plan, and Chapter 7, the business plan financials. Then, in Chapter 8, Applying the Lessons: A Step-by-Step Business-Planning Exercise, we'll give you the opportunity to go through the process for yourself, step by step.

QUESTIONS FOR DISCUSSION: CHAPTER 3

1. Do we really think we are ready to be entrepreneurs on behalf of the people we serve?

2. Do we have enough of the things on the checklist in place to proceed, or do we need to strengthen certain areas? Which are these?

3. Is it important for us to talk through mission and risk every time we engage the business development process, or will annually or semiannually be enough?

4. What business ideas should we consider now? A new business, an expansion?

4

First Steps: Mission Outcomes, Risk, and Idea Generation

OVERVIEW

In this chapter you will learn about the following:

➤ Is the Venture Idea Consistent with Your Mission?
➤ How Much Risk?
➤ What Will the Mission Return Be?
➤ Generating Business Ideas

Now it is time to get to specifics. In this chapter, I'll give you some hands-on practice with the first four steps in the business development process: mission, risk, mission outcomes, and idea generation. While we discussed them briefly in Chapter 3, The Business Development Process, now is the time to get down to specifics. Remember as you read this that you need to *do the steps in order.* Don't skip over or around a step. My experience with hundreds of not-for-profit businesses is that, if you do, you'll be forced to return to the sequence at a later, more expensive, and more disruptive time.

Once (and only after) you have reviewed your mission, examined your willingness to take on risk, and stated your desired mission outcomes are you ready to actually decide what it is that you want to do. While this might seem the most obvious if you are starting a new service from scratch, it is also true for organizations that are thinking about expansions of certain existing services or deletions of others.

❏ FOR EXAMPLE: An organization that ran four drug and alcohol halfway houses (as well as numerous in-school prevention programs) had a dilemma: They had been asked by their primary government funder to start three new facilities in the coming fiscal year in an adjacent community. While they could have simply calculated the costs and agreed to receive funding in the new communities, they decided to first go through the review of mission, their ideas about risk, and to lay out what mission outcomes that they wanted from this expansion. Their initial instincts were to grow by accepting the funding, but as they looked more deeply into what their mission meant, they found that the preventive side had more priority than the intervention side, that the risk of adding new bricks and mortar was much greater than adding school-based programs, and, most importantly, that they could affect more kids' lives if they *didn't* add facility-based programs than if they did, since funds that would have been used to grow the facilities could then be used to expand their preventive efforts.

Again, do the steps in the order I suggest them.

A. IS THE VENTURE IDEA CONSISTENT WITH YOUR MISSION?

As always in a not-for-profit, mission is first. And, as a social entrepreneur, you are all about taking reasonable risks on behalf of your mission. That much we've already covered. But is your mission ready for the risks you are about to embark on? Does the wording and meaning of your charitable mission encompass the idea of social entrepreneurship and, more importantly, does the mission wording include the actual activities your business will generate? By looking at your mission now, you find these things out early, before you go too far. Here's what to do.

1. Review the Mission for Currency

Does your mission statement reflect what you do accurately and completely? Does it describe your service area, your service recipients, and the intent of your mission in total? If it doesn't, you may be subject to Unrelated Business Income Tax.

❑ **FOR EXAMPLE:** Let's imagine a not-for-profit that was formed in 1978 in St. Louis. At the time of its incorporation, the board filed articles of incorporation and an application for charitable status under Section 501(c)(3) of the Internal Revenue Service (IRS) Code. For both of these applications, a charitable purpose had to be included. It read: "To assist African-American youth in St. Louis to achieve educational and employment successes." Since 1978, the organization has grown, and it now serves youth of all ethnic backgrounds in St. Louis, the counties in Missouri that surround St. Louis, and even across the Mississippi River in

East St. Louis, and Belleville, Illinois. Unless someone thought to change the mission statement, this organization could be subject to an Unrelated Business Income Tax review. Why? Because it receives funds for helping children that are not African-American, and it receives funds for helping anyone outside of the city of St. Louis. Both of these exclusions are specifically stated in the mission statement. Thus, a prudent board of directors would change the mission statement to read: "To assist youth in St. Louis and the surrounding communities to achieve educational and employment successes." Of course, if the services the organization provides have changed as well, that should also be addressed.

Make sure you review your mission and charitable purpose carefully for currency. We'll talk at length about Unrelated Business Income Tax in Chapter 10, Technicalities: Unrelated Business Income Tax and Corporate Structuring.

2. Review the Mission for Flexible Language

Does your mission statement allow you to expand what you do, for whom you do it, and where you do it? Is there language in the statement that gives you some entrepreneurial license? For this, you *may* need to remove some geographic or socioeconomic identifiers. The less you limit yourself, the more room you have. Be careful, though, there is a balance here to try to achieve. The fewer identifiers you have, the more generalized you become, the more risk there is of losing focus, losing community and volunteer support. In the preceding example, the organization could keep its donors or volunteers who were committed to youth issues, but runs the risk of alienating its African-American base, at least those who had an ethnic focus rather than a youth focus.

Flexible language is good, but not essential. However, since you are going through a mission review, now is a good time to examine the business flexibility you have in your mission.

3. If Needed, Update the Mission Statement

Examine your mission statement for geographic and socioeconomic exclusions. If they exist, are they current? What about service descriptions? Are they up to date? In both cases, if they are not, amend the mission statement to express the current situation, understanding the trade-off this presents in terms of focus and community support.

Then, make sure you talk about the meaning of the mission as well as just the wording. I wouldn't be surprised if you, your staff, and board members could all recite the wording of your mission. But all too often, the interpretation of those words is very, very different from person to person.

❏ **FOR EXAMPLE:** When I was president of the board of directors of our local Association of Retarded Citizens (ARC), I was in charge of board recruitment. At that time, during the early 1980s, the ARC was rapidly expanding the number of community-based group homes that we ran. Often, these were small homes, with two or three residents, located on residential streets. When I interviewed potential board members, I went through the normal interview process, and then I rattled off our mission statement, which said something to the effect of: "Enable citizens with disabilities to work, live, recreate, and learn to the greatest of their abilities and to participate in and contribute to their community." Nice words. Ones that almost no one could argue with. But then I told the potential board members the following: "What this *means* is that we are constantly buying homes on streets like yours, where two or three people with moderate, or sometimes severe disabilities will live along with house staff. This also means that when we seek to add a home in *your* neighborhood, we expect you to advocate for this with *your* neighbors." The reactions, as you might imagine, ranged from, "Fine, bring 'em on!" to abject horror. But that is the best example I can give of putting it to people about the *meaning* of the mission.

☞ **HANDS ON:** Try this to see how people perceive the meaning of your mission. At your next board meeting, and your next senior staff meeting, distribute a copy of the mission statement to those present. Go over it briefly, perhaps just reading it aloud. Then, ask everyone to write down *the one thing that the organization does that most evidences that mission.* My experience in doing this exercise a hundred times is that, if you have 20 people in the room, you'll get between 18 and 20 different answers. Have people read their answers aloud and, afterward, discuss the reason for the wide-ranging differences in priorities and perceptions. This is a great activity to use to pave the way for a discussion of entrepreneurism and its appropriateness to your organization.

If you do decide to make changes in the mission, such changes require board action and may even require a vote of your full membership, if you have one. Look at your bylaws for guidance. If they are silent on this issue, I suggest that you distribute new draft language in advance to your board, have it discuss any needed changes, and then vote on the changes, along with a rationale for these changes. Record the vote member by member so that you will have that information for the record and to send to the IRS.

4. File the Mission Statement with the Internal Revenue Service

Send the amended mission statement, the rationale for its change, and the date and voting information to the Internal Revenue Service (or Revenue Canada for Canadian readers) for its review and filing. You should get a letter back in approximately three to five months for your files.

☞ **HANDS ON:** Remember, if you don't have a mission statement that is both reflective of what you do *and on file with the IRS,* you could have some very unhappy surprises down the road when your Unrelated Business Income status gets reviewed. Government entities don't care what language you have on the mission statement on your wall. What they do care about is what's in their files.

B. HOW MUCH RISK?

All of us have different genetics when it comes to risk. Some of us thrive on it, some avoid it so adamantly that our behavior becomes risky in itself. Since our organizations are really just groups of people making decisions, this wide variety of risk-taking thresholds extends to our not-for-profits. As a result, some organizations are cavalier in their approach to risk, and some avoid any risk *at all costs* (even to the expense of the mission).

There is no question that the not-for-profit sector is much more risk-averse than the for-profit business world. This is partly due to a culture that says, "It's not your money, don't screw it up, or you might not get any more," and partly due to the ridiculously low capitalization of most not-for-profits (it's tough to risk money you don't have—although people on Wall Street do it every day!). Whatever the reason, it has been my observation that too many not-for-profits let real service opportunities pass because they are not ready to react promptly. Remember, there may be more risk in doing nothing.

But the first step is to find out what the people in your organization think about risk, and find it out early in the process. Now, for example.

☞ **HANDS ON:** Try this well-tested method of finding out your risk quotient. Copy Exhibit 4-1 and hand it out to your board, senior staff, and social entrepreneurial team. Let them fill it out, tally the results, and then discuss the answers. What you will find may be very interesting and will get the issue on the table.

Obviously, the further down this list of choices you go, the higher your organizational willingness to take risks. Don't assume that there is a right

Exhibit 4-1   Internal risk assessment tool.

This form will help your organization assess its willingness and readiness to take risks. Below are four statements. Read all four and then decide which one best describes your view of the most appropriate role for your organization. Please note that even though your organization is a not-for-profit, your staff and board can interpret the role of the organization differently.

Arm of Government: Our organization gets most or all of its funds from some branch of government. As a result, we should provide only the programs that the government asks us to and is willing to pay for.

Government Contractor: One or more branches of government contract with our organization to provide services. Government policy heavily influences us, but we are able to do some things outside of this source of funding.

Local Charity: Our organization should provide the services that our community says that it wants. We know what it wants by what it funds us for, either individually, through United Way, corporate giving, or in fees for services.

Not-for-Profit Business: Our job is to provide services to support our mission. To accomplish this we may accept funds from the government, local or state funders, corporations, individuals, insurers, or others.

I think that the description that best fits our organizations role is (check only one):

	Arm of Government
	Government Contractor
	Local Charity
	Not-for-Profit Business

answer to the survey: There is only your board and staff's answer. And you need to know it now, before you talk through business ideas with any seriousness. The worst thing that can happen is for you not to realize that the staff is full of social entrepreneurs, while the board really sees the organization as an arm of government, or vice versa. Ask now, and you will not only find out where people stand, you will generate discussions that will benefit you throughout the business development process.

C. WHAT WILL THE MISSION RETURN BE?

This is absolutely the good stuff: Here you detail exactly what you want the return on investment from your new business or expansion to be in terms of mission. You need to write down what mission outcomes you want from the business in two different ways: mission that comes from the business itself, and mission that comes from any profits the business might earn.

❏ **FOR EXAMPLE:** A sheltered workshop that seeks to employ people with disabilities starts a janitorial service that cleans offices. The business has two mission outcomes: the 14 jobs for people with disabilities that the business will generate, and a projected profit of about $17,000 per year starting in the second year. The organization decides that half of this money will be kept in the business to expand and grow, and the other half will go to paying for children with disabilities to go to summer camp. While the not-for-profit was not exactly sure how much profit it would earn prior to doing its business plan, it committed half of any profits to the summer camp scholarship fund.

The idea in this step is to assure that you set a high bar for yourself and your organization in terms of mission outcome. Why do this? Why commit yourself so early in the process? Because it accomplishes two things. First, it motivates your staff and board to want to do the major amount of work required to develop a new business. Second, it keeps you on the straight and narrow from the earliest days of the process. You stay focused on mission, as you should.

As I have already said, in all investments of your resources, you need to look at your financial return as well as your mission return. This step helps you identify your goals for those returns. Understand that you almost certainly will have to modify your mission outcome goals as you move through the business development process. Even so, it is important to do this step now, and to keep the outcomes that you desire as focused as possible on *direct provision of service.*

☞ **HANDS ON:** Try to avoid the temptation to not be specific in your goal setting, or worse, to set a goal that is not directly related to mission. While it is very likely that what your business does will provide direct mission, what you do with any profits is more up in the air, and the temptation for many management teams is to target the earnings on important, but not direct mission, uses. Sending children to summer camp is easily identifiable as a direct mission outcome. Fixing the roof, paving the parking lot, putting new tires on the agency vehicles, buying a new phone system, or paying down debt, while all laudable activities, are not *directly* mission related. Do these activities support the mission indirectly? Sure. Do they motivate people to work harder? Doubtful. Try your best to keep the mission outcomes direct and personal.

☞ **HANDS ON:** One way to do this step even better is to let your line staff develop a listing of things that are needed in the community that could be uses of your profits. Then the SE team can use the list to pick something that is high-mission priority, and the staff who suggested things will have more ownership. One way I have seen this done is to distribute a memo to staff, or discuss at staff meetings, asking how they would spend $100, $1,000, and $10,000 on direct mission for the people you serve. Then, separate lists of small, medium, and large items are developed from which the ultimate choice is made.

D. GENERATING BUSINESS IDEAS

Now we get to the meat of the matter: What is it exactly that you are going to do? What new service will you provide, what new population will you serve, what new level of growth will you attempt? The answer to this question is obviously critical to your success or failure, and so you need to proceed cautiously.

☞ **HANDS ON:** *Stop!* If you think you have already finished this step, don't leave now! Never assume that an idea that you assume will work will, *especially if it is an expansion of an existing service.* In reviewing hundreds of business-planning failures, the ones I see most often are *failures to plan at all* when it comes to an expansion of a service. Agency after agency decided that they could do more service as well as they did the existing amount. First bad assumption. Then they also decided that what they did well here, they could do well there. Second bad assumption. As I told you earlier, there is no guarantee that you will succeed in location B just because you have succeeded in location A. Thus, it is important that you go through the entire business idea development process. You will get a better set of ideas to work from. And, if your original idea proves the best, you will be able to initiate it with a much higher likelihood of success.

In developing potential business ideas you will try to identify something that you can do (an area where you have or can quickly acquire a core competence) for someone who wants the service. As you go through the idea generation process, make sure you remember this all-important rule:

> *It doesn't matter if the idea makes sense to you, what matters is if it makes sense to your market. Is there a market for* what *you want to sell,* how *you want to sell it,* where *and* when *you want to sell it, and for the* price *you want to charge?*

If not, then the idea will almost certainly fail.

There are two parts to the idea generation process: brainstorming to get a list of possible businesses or new services, and then developing a set of criteria to sort through your ideas and narrow them down to the best two or three for your organization. The idea is to start with lots of ideas, not just one or two. Where do you get lots of ideas? Simple. From your staff and board.

☞ **HANDS ON:** Convene a brainstorming session of staff, board, even outsiders who understand your mission, know your willingness to take risks, and what the mission use of your profits will be. Ask what you can do well to serve people, make money, meet a market want, move into a new market, and so forth. You will be surprised at how many ideas people will have—they have been thinking of them for years, but probably have never been asked. Make sure to have a facilitator who understands that this is brainstorming—not the time to judge or criticize ideas. In an hour to an hour-and-half meeting, most brainstorming groups generate 30 to 60 ideas. Just have the facilitator write the ideas down on a flip chart, and ask questions to make sure he or she fully understands the idea. But absolutely no "dumping" on ideas or the idea generator!

Depending on the size of your staff, board, and the number of outsiders you include, you may need more than one meeting. The best group size for brainstorming is about 20 to 25 people. More than that and people don't get to contribute; less and there is not enough critical neural mass in the room to get going.

How do you narrow all these great (and some awful) ideas down to the best few? After all the group meetings are complete, you can do that by developing what I refer to as *business criteria.* Use your social entrepreneur team to decide on the criteria by which you will sort your many ideas. These criteria may focus on outcomes, investment limits, mission, or whatever you think is important. The key is that these criteria allow you to have an objective way to decide which two or three ideas to pursue and allow everyone in the organization to know what is important as they continue to generate new ideas for you.

Some examples of criteria (and business ideas) are shown on the following pages. The first example, shown in Exhibit 4-2, comes from an organization that employed people with disabilities. Across the top you can see the business options that they were considering, and down the left-hand side are the criteria they set. They chose to rate each item on a yes, no, or not applicable (N/A) basis, but you could do it on a numerical scale

Exhibit 4-2   Rating of possible business ventures—sheltered workshop.

Criteria	Foam Packaging	Film Shrink	Wood Products	Rest Areas	Comm. Services	Industrial Custodial	Maid Services
Serves mission of agency	yes	yes	yes	yes	yes	yes	yes
Space available	yes	no	no	N/A	yes	N/A	yes
Low start-up costs ($5,000)	no	no	no	yes	yes	no	no
Can begin in six months	yes	no	no	no	yes	yes	no
Internal knowledge of product/service	yes	no	yes	yes	yes	yes	yes
Resources available	yes	no	maybe	yes	yes	yes	yes
Drain on staff	yes	yes	yes	yes	yes	yes	yes
Potential profitability	good	good	?	fair	good	good	very good
Major risk of failure	no	yes	yes	no	no	yes	no
Competition	no	no	yes	state	no	yes	yes ?
Resentment by for-profits in the area	no	no	yes	no	no	If too large, yes	maybe
Realistic growth	yes	yes	?	yes	yes	yes	probable
Identified market, need, or opportunity	yes	no	no	yes	yes	yes	available
Realistic opportunity	yes	?	?	yes	yes	yes	?
Priority rank	1	5	5	3	2	4	7

(1–5, for example) or an alphabetic rating (A–F), or however you feel works best for your organization and social entrepeneur team.

In this case, the choice was to pursue foam packaging first, commercial services second, and a rest area cleaning contract third.

Exhibit 4-3 shows a different organization, a children's museum, its business ideas, and its criteria. Its scale was 0 to 5 with 5 being the best rating to go ahead, and 0 being the worst. Thus, a rating of 0 on competition means that there is a lot of competition.

As you can see, the highest scores were found for developing school-based programs, contracting with day care providers, and expanding hours. In this case, the museum staff would take the top two or three and develop preliminary feasibility studies on them, which we will cover in the next chapter.

You don't need to use the criteria in the preceding examples. Use ones that are important to your social entrepreneur team. By developing criteria that help you evaluate your many expansion and business ideas, you will be more consistent and more objective than if you just go with your gut.

Exhibit 4-3   Rating of possible business ventures—children's museum.

Criteria	School-Based Programs	Expand Hours	All-Night Birthday Parties	Publication/ Software Development	Hire Full-Time Developer	Additional Site	Contracts with Day Care Providers
Serves mission of agency	5	5	3	4	1	5	4
Less than $15,000 investment	5	2	5	1	0	0	3
Serves children directly	5	5	5	4	0	5	5
Do we have the skill?	4	5	2	1	0	5	4
Affects other services	2	2	5	3	3	3	3
Identified want	5	2	5	1	5	3	4
Profitable in three years	2	5	3	0	5	2	4
Feeds other services	5	4	2	1	0	3	4
Examples to follow?	5	0	2	0	5	5	5
Competition	3	3	2	0	0	2	3
Problem with funders/donors	2	4	4	1	5	5	5
Supports StrategicPlan	5	5	1	2	5	3	2
Total Score	**48**	**42**	**39**	**18**	**29**	**41**	**46**

☞ **HANDS ON:** Whatever you do, *don't* have only one person do this evaluation. The only way to benefit from the objectivity that this process allows you is to have the entire team fill out the criteria sheet on their own, and then add up or average the scores. Discuss the results, including why the highest-scoring ideas were rated so high. This will build a better understanding and, hopefully, agreement among the social entrepreneur team about which kinds of businesses or expansions make the most sense. You'll need that level of understanding as the organization moves toward becoming more and more entrepreneurial.

During my years as a consultant, it has been interesting to watch people develop and use their business criteria. The same thing happens almost every time. It works like this. Most of the agencies I help come into the business development process with a "great" idea, or to be kinder, a favorite idea. Never, I repeat, *never,* in all of those cases, have I seen an agency go through the idea generation process, develop and apply business criteria, and *end up with the highest-rated idea being the one that they started with as their favorite.* Think about it—*before* you push ahead with your favorite (great?) project. Develop the business criteria and utilize them the way they were intended to be used, as a group.

Now you have completed the first four steps in the business development process, ones that bring you to the threshold of the first major work effort in the process: the feasibility study. By doing all four of the steps in order, and not just jumping ahead to the point of idea generation or to developing a feasibility study, you have laid an important foundation not only for your pursuit of your current project, but also for the development of your organization into a more entrepreneurial not-for-profit.

Remember that while the process may, in your mind, slow you down, it really allows everyone in the organization to come along with you. You may be ready to leap ahead, to jump off of the proverbial entrepreneurial cliff, but many others won't be so eager to risk their careers with you. By talking at length about your mission, by getting a better understanding of each other's willingness to take risk, by declaring and defining a clear mission outcome early in the process, you'll bring more people along with you on your entrepreneurial journey. Then, by including a large number of people in the business idea development stage, you increase their understanding and ownership of the process, which is crucial if you want the organization to become and stay entrepreneurial.

So now we know more about your mission, more about how much risk you want to take, we have some specific mission outcomes and a bunch of good ideas that have gone through our business criteria sieve. But which idea is best, and will it meet the lofty goals you have set? Finding out is a new job, one that requires a new tool: the feasibility study, which is the subject of our next chapter.

RECAP

In this chapter, we have covered the all-important first four steps in the business development process which are as follows:

1. Review your mission.
2. Establish the risk willingness of your organization.
3. Establish the mission outcomes of the business.
4. Idea generation.

You read how important it is to have a clear understanding of your mission statement, and to have it reflect accurately what your organization does, who it serves, and where it does its good works. We went over the process of finding out how much risk you, your staff, and board are willing to take, and I provided you with a short internal self-assessment tool. Then we turned to the crucial step of defining a mission outcome, both for the business itself, and for any profits the business might generate. I emphasized how crucial it is for you to be specific and define some direct mission benefits for the business if you want to generate and maintain board and staff support for this project.

Finally, we looked at how to generate a lot of business ideas, using your staff and volunteers. Even though you may have one primary idea at this point, it is important to ask people what they think to increase their understanding of the process, to increase their ownership in the outcomes, and, most importantly, because you will almost certainly get some really excellent ideas. I showed you how to sort and sift those ideas by developing business criteria, and we looked at two examples of such criteria.

Only now, after going through these four steps are you ready to proceed to the feasibility study stage, which begins in the next chapter.

QUESTIONS FOR DISCUSSION: CHAPTER 4

1. Is our mission statement sufficiently up to date? Does it reflect what we do, where we do it, and who we serve?

2. Do we have a consistent understanding of what our mission statement means on a day-to-day basis?

3. How much risk are we willing to take? Should we use Peter's risk assessment tool?

4. What are some ideas for mission outcomes? What would we do with a $10,000 profit? A $50,000 one?

5. How can we best involve people in developing ongoing business ideas so that we can become more entrepreneurial?

5

Feasibility Studies

OVERVIEW

In this chapter you will learn about the following:

- ➤ The Purpose of Feasibility Studies
- ➤ Preliminary Feasibility Studies
- ➤ The Final Feasibility Study

By this point, assuming that you are reading this book in order, you will have reviewed and perhaps amended you mission statement, looked at your organizational risk-taking quotient, established some motivational mission outcomes for your profits, developed a large list of possible business or expansion activities, developed some business criteria, and used those criteria to sort through all the business ideas to get at the best two or three.

Whew! That's a lot of activity, but not much real business planning. You've done so much but, really, you know so little, at least at this point. Don't believe me? Let's look at the many, many important things you haven't yet found out.

You don't yet know much about the business industry you are considering, its markets, its advantages and disadvantages, its costs, and its long-term potential for providing mission, and possible profits. You don't know what the customers of this kind of business want, and whether the capabilities of your organization can be focused enough to meet those wants. You don't know about competition, who they are, where they are, and what their focus is. You don't yet know about any environmental, administrative, regulatory, or other issues that might pertain to the business.

All of these issues are important, even critical, to your potential for success and to reducing your entrepreneurial risk to a reasonable one for your organization. Remember, even if your new venture is an expansion of something you have already done, a service in which you are expert, you don't know the answers yet for the new population or new community that you may be considering serving, and they may well be different answers than those that you are used to. Even if you are just going to grow right where you are, doing more of the same service for the same population group, you don't know if you can do a *lot* more of what you do *well*.

❑ **FOR EXAMPLE:** A friend of mine (who we'll call Mike) runs a mental health center that had found a niche in family counseling. Their eight counselors were highly trained in resolving family conflict, in interventions, and a variety of other services that they had developed over the years. These counselors, all of whom had at least 10 years on the job, had full case loads just from word-of-mouth referrals from former clients, from ministers, the police, teachers, and other affected individuals. The family counseling program was successful, well thought of in the community, and on top of everything, modestly profitable. It supported other programs of the center that could not totally pay their own way and was one of the big bricks in the financial foundation of the organization.

Mike decided to make the brick bigger, by doubling the number of counselors over 18 months and actively selling the services through flyers, advertising, and calling potential referral sources. He assumed that, in his words, "what we were doing well, we could do a lot of well." He was wrong. By adding counselors who were not as experienced and not used to the system of interventions needed to maintain the success rates that the organization had enjoyed, quality and reputation suffered. Internally, the human resources systems couldn't support the additional counselors and their support people. The information management system was strained, and Mike had also not anticipated the amount of new cash (called working capital) he would need to invest in his receivables.

The entire episode took three years from inception until everyone realized that the organization's reach had exceeded its grasp. It took four more years for the organization to recover financially. Mike will tell you that he should have really taken the time to look into all of the effects of such rapid growth, "If we had done a real feasibility study instead of just barging ahead assuming we knew everything, a lot of this pain and frustration could have been avoided."

You need to take the time to do your feasibility studies. I'll say the same thing about your business plan when we get to that chapter; the idea of the process is to help you reduce your risk to an acceptable level. If you don't use the tools that are designed to reduce that risk, the risk will remain. There is too much you don't know at this stage. Use the feasibility study process to help you fill those information holes.

A. THE PURPOSE OF FEASIBILITY STUDIES

Feasibility studies are intended to answer this question: *Can we provide this service (or make this product) in this market, at this price, with the resources we can muster, and meet both our mission and financial goals?* At this point in the process, the answer to that question is very unclear, and the result could go either way. Remember the purpose of feasibility studies is to see if it makes sense to move ahead with this particular idea now. The purpose is *not* to rationalize proceeding no matter what. All of which means that you need to go into the process with an open mind, and let the information you will gather guide your opinions, not the other way around.

If done correctly, the preliminary and final feasibility studies will tell you if and under what conditions it makes sense to proceed. It will give you and your SE team a much better idea of how much financial and mission outcome you can expect from your new business or service expansion.

There are two kinds of feasibility studies: *preliminary* and *final*. The preliminary is just what its name implies, an early look at the feasibility of an idea. Preliminary studies are short and focus on just a few key areas of information. You will probably want to do preliminary feasibility studies on the top two or three ideas that made it through your business criteria review.

Final feasibility studies are done on ideas that make it through the preliminary phase. These are longer and more detailed, and when you are done with your final feasibility study, much of the information you will need to write your business plan is gathered, and much of the focus for the business has been defined.

Let's look at what is in each kind of study.

B. PRELIMINARY FEASIBILITY STUDIES

The idea of doing a preliminary feasibility study is to help you decide whether your initial ideas about the business make sense in the current market environment. The study should be short, three to five pages long, and only take a few days of work to complete. Since you will want to develop preliminary feasibility studies on more than one of your ideas, it makes sense to take a quick look at each rather than going into one in great detail. Keeping the preliminary study short also makes it easier for you to abandon a bad idea now rather than "going just a little further" on an idea that has taken up more time and research.

There are really just four things that you need to do in your preliminary feasibility study. They are the following:

1. Define what your product or service is.

2. Determine whether your target customer will want this service or product.

3. Explore the industry of which your service or product is part.

4. Make sure that your organization has the core competencies necessary to do the job well from day one.

By doing these four tasks, you will have a better sense of whether your venture idea and your organization are a good fit, and whether you should proceed with an idea to the final feasibility step. Let's look at each of the four tasks in some more detail.

1. Define What Your Product or Service Is

This step sounds so easy. It's harder than you may think, and getting it right is crucial to your being able to assess feasibility. Without an accurate description of your service or product you will not be able to focus on who your target markets are, and thus on what those markets want from your organization, you won't be able to define what core competencies you need, you won't be able to generate accurate sales projections, budgets, or even a list of what might go wrong in your new business or expansion. In short, without a good service or product definition, you can't write a feasibility study or a business plan. So let's examine how to write such a definition.

You need to pare down your service or product to its essentials, be as specific as possible, strip away jargon and generalities, and resist the urge to globalize and exaggerate.

❏ FOR EXAMPLE: Here is a service description that you may have seen. *Help prevent teen pregnancy through training and counseling.* Okay. So what? How can you measure your markets, discover what they want, figure out where they are and how to reach them? What if you want to expand your services? Is your objective to do more counseling or prevent more pregnancies? Is this agency going to prevent pregnancy all over the planet or just in North America? How will it provide this service? Where? When? With what kind of staff?

Now let's look at the service and add the same thing that a reporter would in writing a story: *who, what, where, when,* and *how.* Our new service description might be as follows: *Provide training and counseling to junior high and high school students in three local high schools at lunch and after school using trained staff and peer volunteers.* Now we know so much more about the idea. We can estimate the size of the staff needed; we can find out the number of students who could possibly be counseled; we can record the number of pregnancies before and after our intervention; we can figure out a budget for travel, supplies, audio visual equipment, and so forth.

By knowing more specifically what we will do, we can much better figure out how we are going to do it, and, just as importantly, whether we have the capacity to do the service well.

❏ **FOR EXAMPLE:** Here are some good and not-so-good service descriptions:

Good: Provide museum exhibits in 12 local elementary schools four times a year.

Not So Good: Serve families with children 12 and under. (Note: "Families with children 12 and under" is a *great* target market identification, but not a service description.)

Good: Clean and resell used clothing to low-income individuals that live within five miles of our new store.

Not So Good: Run another thrift shop.

Good: Run a weekly support group for up to 20 children of divorce using trained counselors in our church all-purpose room.

Not So Good: Have a divorce support ministry.

I hope you get the idea: The more specific the better, understanding that, at this point, the idea is still in the preliminary stages of development. As you progress into the final feasibility study and perhaps even on to a full business plan, you will almost certainly need to amend and refine your service description.

2. Determine Whether Your Target Customer Will Want This Service or Product

Even though this is just a preliminary study, you need to start the process of delineating the difference between what you *think* people want and what you *know* they want. And, the only way to know is to ask. So ask at least a few people who would use (or pay for) the service *as specifically as possible* about your new idea, and whether it would be something that would interest them enough to utilize it. Remember what I said in the last chapter, the core question is: Do people want the service or product you will provide when you will provide it, where you will provide it, how you will provide it, and for the price you will provide it? If the answer to any one of those items is no, your idea will not succeed. Now is the time to find out, so ask!

☞ **HANDS ON:** You may want to poll people by phone or in person. Let's suppose you were a staff person at the church considering the support group for kids of divorce that was outlined in the preceding list of services. You might identify 10 to 15 divorced couples (either members of your church, or in your neighborhood), and call them. A typical call might sound something like this:

"Hi, I'm from the XYZ church, and we're thinking of starting a new weekly support group for kids who have had a divorce in their family. We're trying to get an idea of interest in this service. As we see it, the meetings would be weekly for about and hour and a half at the church, with a trained counselor. The child could come for as many sessions as he or she wanted to, and we see a cost of between $5 and $10 per session. Is this something that you might be interested in? Do you have any ideas on how to improve this service? Thanks!"

By doing this kind of polling, you will not only get a feel for local interest, you'll probably get some excellent ideas about the idea. In fact, a client of mine used this exact method for this exact idea and was told that the organization should run three groups, one for 5- to 9-year-olds, one for 10- to 13-year-olds, and one for high school kids. They also received ideas on the best time of day and eventually set up groups for kids with their parents as well. The lesson: Call and ask.

I understand that in order to make my time line of just a few days for your preliminary feasibility studies, you don't have time to do a written survey, but you *do* have time to call, and this early kind of market assessment is key to the decision about whether to proceed with your idea to a final feasibility study. What if no one wants the service? What if everyone wants it, but no one wants to pay? What if the service is already available down the street? What if everyone thinks that the idea is great, but the planned location is a real loser? Take the time to call, ask, and then *really* listen!

3. Explore the Industry of Which Your Service or Product Is a Part

Now it is time to take a look at your industry. This step is intended to let you find out the trends in your chosen industry and to evaluate how they will affect you. Questions you will ask might include the following: Is the industry growing or declining? Is it fragmented (lots of providers) or consolidating? Is it moving toward certification or accreditation? Is it staying local or going regional or national? How is the increased use of technology and communications changing the industry? What regulations and regulatory agencies are pertinent? Is it labor-intensive, capital-intensive, or both? What are the characteristics of success in this kind of business? You need to assess whether this industry is one you want to be in.

☞ **HANDS ON:** Remember, even if your idea is to expand an existing service, and you think you know everything about the industry since you are already in it, you should take a few hours to go through this step. Get on the phone with your trade association at the local, state, or national level and talk through the trends in the industry, what the association sees for the next two or three years, and ask for the names of two or three independent experts in the field to talk to. Call the experts up and pick their brains for 20 minutes or so. The idea here is to avoid staying in an industry that is moving away from your ability to continue to provide excellent services.

❑ **FOR EXAMPLE:** I work with a large number of organizations whose mission is to work with people with disabilities. At least five of these organizations have decided in the past three years to get out of the provision of residential services and focus on day treatment, employment, recreation, or some other set of services. Residential care, as an industry, is much more regulated, more expensive, and very difficult to keep staffed. Each of these decisions to abandon the service to another provider was made after the agency developed a feasibility study on expanding its residential services. In other words, in considering adding group homes, the agencies decided to get out of the area completely because of what they saw coming over the horizon. Not an easy decision, nor one that they took lightly.

☞ **HANDS ON:** If you need to find the trade association for your new industry, your local library will probably have a copy of *The Encyclopedia of Trade Associations*. This publication lists all the trade associations by industry and state. Once you find the right association, call it and ask about your idea. Many trade associations have packets of information on how to get into business, regulations to meet, and so forth. They also can tell you about trade publications to read and provide you with a list of experts with whom to consult. Trade associations can be terrific resources, so call them!

4. Make Sure That Your Organization Has the Core Competencies Necessary to Do the Job Well from Day One

Look at your organization in the light of what you have found so far. Can you match up things that you do really, really well (your core competencies) with the wants of this new market? If you can't, you either need to develop the competencies ASAP, or try a different market. Remember the organizational chart that I showed you in Chapter 2, The Benefits of the Social Entrepreneurism Model, the one where the agency did a little of everything, just because there was a grant? Don't do that. Find a match between wants and competencies. And if there is none, move on to another venture idea.

Once you have gone through these steps, write up a brief report that lists your service description, what you found out from your calls to potential customers, and what you discovered from your review of the industry. Then, from the two or three ideas that you ran through the preliminary feasibility process, select the best one to use as you develop a full feasibility study.

❏ **FOR EXAMPLE:** A Florida university looked into three ventures that would serve as potential vehicles for investment and job creation in the Indochinese refugee community of a northern Florida city. Businesses selected for evaluation had to meet the following criteria: (1) A quick start-up, (2) jobs require a low level of proficiency in the English language, (3) relatively little start-up capital required and (4) successful operation within the existing regulatory climate including local, state, and federal regulations. After evaluating the three business venture ideas based on the criteria listed, the university was able to eliminate two of the ideas and settle on one venture for the development of a final feasibility study. The proposed business was to develop a janitorial service for local businesses.

C. THE FINAL FEASIBILITY STUDY

The final feasibility study allows you to assess whether your idea is feasible given your resources and your long-term and short-term financial and mission goals for the business. For example, if you need the new venture or expansion to provide services to 500 people a year, the plan should allow for that. If, on the other hand, you need to have a $50,000 profit in three years to support another program, the study should show that this has to occur.

❏ **FOR EXAMPLE:** A 30,000-acre wildlife refuge was considering allowing paid camping in one corner of the property to supplement the income of the refuge and to provide an easily available source of customers for tours and educational materials that were sold at the refuge headquarters. The feasibility study showed that the camping area could be developed in such a manner as to have minimal effect on the wildlife, and the initial investment would be paid back in three years, after which projected sizable profits could go toward acquiring additional adjacent land to expand the refuge. The key to board approval of the project (and its hefty initial investment) was demonstrating that deferring the purchase of some land now (with the investment money) would result in the purchase of much more land later, as well as more exposure to the refuge by people (campers) who would not otherwise have seen it. Thus, the development of clear, desired outcomes before the feasibility study began helped the organization's board be more comfortable with its weighty decision.

Which brings me to another point: These are important decisions and not ones that you should rush the board through. The more you involve at least some of your governing volunteers in the feasibility process, the more comfortable they will be later: Keep them at least somewhat involved in each step.

☞ **HANDS ON:** To develop your feasibility study have the social entrepreneur team members who worked on your preliminary feasibility studies each take one area of the final feasibility to work on. For example, one person might flesh out the data on the industry, while another does more in-depth customer surveys. A third might gather information on start-up and operating costs, and a fourth could develop the income and expense and cash flow worksheets. The effort involved in a final feasibility study is quite long and hard, so split up the work so that no one individual is overly burdened, while at the same time broadening ownership of the plan and the understanding of the business challenges.

Final Feasibility Study Contents

Your final feasibility study needs to have the following sections in it as outlined in Exhibit 5-1. I've included some critical questions that should be considered and answered in each of those sections. Not every question will relate to your new business or expansion, but try to answer as many as you can. *I have emphasized the most crucial questions in italics.*

☞ **HANDS ON:** Feel free to add questions to this list that make the feasibility study your own. You may have certain regulations, accreditation rules, or funder requirements to meet. Additionally, your board may establish higher thresholds or specific benchmarks that need to be met before you proceed to the business plan.

Exhibit 5-1   Final feasibility contents.

INTRODUCTION
Statement on the business
Can you define precisely what this new business or expansion will do?
Who will operate the business? Do they have the skills and experience to run it?
How will it benefit your mission and the organization?
What are the characteristics of successful businesses of this type?
Will it operate within your present corporate structure or will you spin off the business venture into a separate corporation?

Information on industry
What changes are taking place in the industry?
Are there trends within the industry that you can take advantage of, or others that could negatively affect your service?
What makes your service or product different from the competition?
How will you manage a drop off in demand?

Information on competitors
Who is the competition?
Where are they located?
How will you compete?
Is there enough of a market to support you and the competition?
How does your price compare with your competitors' prices?
Can you price competitively and still make money?
If your price is higher, what additional value do you provide to your customers?

Start-up capital
How much start-up capital do you need?
Where will you get it?

Basics on pricing
How will you arrive at the price you charge?
Are you locked into one price or do you have a variety of payers and price scales?

MARKET INFORMATION
Potential markets
Who is(are) the target market(s) for this business?
How will you inform the people you want to serve within this market(s)?
What is your plan to find out what your target market wants?
What is your sales strategy?

Exhibit 5-1   Continued

Market research
Have you polled potential customers to find out what they want from a
*   business of this type?*
What are your survey results?

Wants and needs
Is there both a need and a want for your product or service? How do you
    know?
Do potential customers want this product or service when, where, how,
    and for the price you plan to provide it?
If so, how do you know? What is your estimate of the demand?

Hurdles and pitfalls
What problems could arise in the operation of this business venture and
*   how will you overcome them?*
Are there some problems that cannot be resolved?

ASSUMPTIONS ABOUT THE SIZE OF THE BUSINESS
How large an operation will this be in terms of such items as budget and
*   staffing to start?*
If rapid growth comes sooner than expected, can you handle it?
Can you access the cash to let you afford growth?
What will you do if your estimates of growth are not accurate?
Is a business that earns a small profit—or no profit at all—worth operat-
    ing? Is there enough mission outcome to justify the investment?

START-UP COSTS
What are your initial start-up costs? Will you require such things as
    licenses, telephones, office supplies, insurance, and advertising costs?
How long will you operate before you begin to generate net income?

PRO FORMA FINANCIALS
What are your break-even projections per month and per year?
How long will it take you to reach your break-even numbers?
Can you afford to lose money for that long a period of time?
Do you have a projection of income and expense for three years, and a
    cash flow projection for three years?

DISCUSSION OF FEASIBILITY
Is this business or expansion feasible at this point for your organization?
Does it meet your mission goals?

Exhibit 5-1   Continued

Is the risk acceptable?
Is there a better place to invest your money and time?
Can you compete with the competition?
Is the market growing or shrinking and how will this affect your organization?
Can you maintain quality?
Will you alienate potential customers if growth occurs too quickly?
Will it be possible for you to maintain quality control if rapid growth occurs?

RECAP

In this chapter, we have looked at the feasibility study process, both the why and the how. We went through the best ways to develop a preliminary feasibility study in a few days, and I gave you both an outline and a long list of questions to ask in developing your final feasibility study. But I want to, just one more time, put the feasibility study in the context of the complete business development process. I know, from long experience, that there are readers who skipped the first few chapters to get to here. If you are one of those, read this list of the entire process, and then go back and start at the beginning, please, for your own sake.

Review of the Business Development Process

Step 1. Review your mission statement
         Is it the one you want?
         Does the IRS have a copy?
         Is the business related or unrelated?

Step 2. Do an internal risk analysis
         How much risk are you willing to take?

Step 3. Define the mission-based outcomes of your business
         Specific outcomes for the people you serve
         Use of profits

Step 4. Idea generation
         Brainstorming
         Social entrepreneur team
         Establish criteria
         Narrow ideas to two or three

Step 5. Feasibility studies

> Preliminary
> Define the product/service
> Define market
> Define market wants
> Explore industry
> Rating of business ventures
> Select one business venture
>
> Final
> Introduction
> Market/product/service information
> Assumptions about size and organization
> Start-up costs
> Pro forma financials
> Discussion of feasibility

After all of this, you can move to the development of a full business plan. And, as you move ahead to developing a business plan, remember that the feasibility studies you have completed are designed to reduce your risk but not eliminate it. You still need to develop a business plan, which is the subject of our next chapter. And, remember that if your feasibility study showed that your idea for a new service or expansion is not feasible, don't proceed! If you do, you throw out all the risk reduction that the process is supposed to provide you.

QUESTIONS FOR DISCUSSION: CHAPTER 5

1. How many ideas should we take through the preliminary feasibility study process?

2. Is there a way to standardize our use of this process for all our business decisions, even decisions to extend our services into a new fiscal year?

3. How can we customize the list of questions that Peter offers in the final feasibility study to meet our needs best?

4. What role should our board have in this part of the process? What about including outsiders?

6

The Business Plan

OVERVIEW

In this chapter you will learn about the following:

> ➤ The Need for a Business Plan
> ➤ The Contents of the Business Plan
> ➤ A Sample Business Plan

Now it is time to get to the grunt work of the venture development process: the business plan. This is really the culmination of all your efforts in developing ideas, assessing risk, looking at ideas, asking markets what they want, matching up wants with core capabilities, and evaluating feasibility of your ideas. In this chapter, we'll look at the business plan, why it is important, what the outcomes of a good plan should be, how to write it, and then examine a case study business plan.

Not all of your business plans will need to be long or involved. For example, the use of business techniques to evaluate whether your organization should continue with a specific program might well be shorter and simpler than the examples included here. But, as I said earlier, if you are to be a successful social entrepreneur, you need to know how, why, and when to write a business plan. This chapter and the next on business plan financials will show you how.

A. THE NEED FOR A BUSINESS PLAN

Boy, do I hear a lot of complaining from my social entrepreneur clients on this one: "Why do we need to write a business plan?" Why do they complain? Because, like you, they have already done a great deal of work on their potential venture, and they want to get on with the business, not spend more time sitting in front of a word processor and spreadsheet. The attitude of these people is understandable, so let's look at all you, your staff, and social entrepreneur team should have done by now in the business-planning process:

- Reviewed your mission
- Looked at your willingness to take risk
- Planned what the mission outcome of your venture will be and what you will do with your profits
- Selected a business idea
- Performed a preliminary feasibility study
- Prepared a final feasibility study

That's a lot of work, so why do another document? Why go through all the extra effort? For a number of reasons, not the least of which is to further reduce your risk. Let's look at three core reasons in order of importance.

1. *Writing a business plan forces you to take an objective, critical, less-emotional look at your business project in its entirety.* One more time: The purpose of business planning is to help you reduce your risk to a reasonable level. And here is your last shot at maximizing your risk reduction. By going through the development of a complete business plan and not just stopping with a feasibility study, you get one more look at the entire business idea in context, with more detailed financials, and that should allow you to make the best decision possible regarding whether to go ahead. I know I have told you repeatedly that being a social entrepreneur is all about taking risk, but I have always added that the risk should be *reasonable* given your unique organizational situation. Write the plan.

2. *The finished product is an operating tool that, if properly used, will help you manage your business and work toward its success.* Way, way, *way* too many not-for-profit managers just keep adding duties as their organization expands. Remember the organizational chart I showed you in Chapter 2, The Benefits of the Social Entrepreneurism Model, the one where the not-for-profit had grown from one business into many as it chased grants? I'll guarantee you that, as it added different entities, the executive director tried to manage all of the diverse businesses him- or herself. And, to understate, that is not smart. First, as an executive director, you already have a full plate of things to do. Delegation is a crucial skill and a necessity if you are going to do your job well. Second, you simply cannot be expert in 10 different industries. So, how do you assure that your new venture will get implemented properly without you actually running it on a day-to-day basis? Ta-da! Use your business plan. Not only should it include your assumptions about the markets, resources, and the like, it should include goals and objectives that allow you to monitor the person who is supervising the venture

directly. Thus, the business plan becomes a contract between you and your board, and then between you and the venture manager, who *should* be an expert, or at least experienced, in the kind of business you are starting or expanding.

3. *The completed business plan is the best means of communicating your ideas to others.* The old saw goes as follows: the business plan is the language of business. And, like so many pieces of "old" wisdom, it is true. Not only does your business plan reduce your risk and provide a delegation tool, it really is the best way to communicate your entire idea to a wide variety of people, including your board and your potential financing resources.

❏ **FOR EXAMPLE:** Let's say I am one of your board members and you come to me with a great idea for expanding your organization's transportation services into an adjacent county. You talk a great line and are an excellent manager. No matter, my answer will be, "Show me your business plan."

❏ **FOR EXAMPLE:** Once you convince your board that the expansion is merited, you have to finance all sorts of new vehicles. You go to the bank, again with a great idea, and the approval of your board in hand. What will it say? You guessed it, "Show us your business plan."

❏ **FOR EXAMPLE:** Now that you have your vehicles, you still have some problems with cash flow for the first few months, since your major state funder takes a while to get its payments on line and in the mail. You go to your major fuel supplier with the following news: "We are doubling our transportation program and will double our fuel purchases. You've been great to us, but we need some help to make the plan work. I know that we have paid you in 30 days up until now, but for the next six months, we need to pay you in 60 days, until our funding streams get fully on line. Then we'll go back to 30 days." What will the fuel supplier say? Right. "Show me your business plan."

So, take the time to develop the plan. You've put in so much work to this point. Finish the job, and get the full benefit of your investment of time and effort.

B. THE CONTENTS OF THE BUSINESS PLAN

A business plan consists of several important parts. You need to have all of them at least in some form for you to have a true business plan. Let's look at each of them individually.

A title page identifying the business plan as the property of your organization. This cover letter includes your organization's name, address, and telephone number and the month and the year that the plan was written or revised. One paragraph should state in simple terms who the business plan belongs to and the limitations on its distribution. Remember, this is your plan, your property, and should not be freely handed out without your knowledge and permission.

A table of contents. The sad fact is that, even if you write like Hemingway, not everyone who reads the plan will read all of it. So, let your readers know where the various parts of the plan are to help them focus efficiently.

A summary of the plan. This part should come early, but be written last. It should include a brief paragraph about each of the major sections of the plan including the description of your organization; a succinct description of the product or service; a short description of the market; a brief paragraph on production and one on distribution, if needed; a short paragraph on the financing requirements; and a time line for implementation.

A description of your organization and its business. You need to describe your organization in this area. Why are you in this business? What is your core service or product? What experience do you have in the market you are going after? Will there be any reorganization to facilitate this business? How will you handle growth? What competencies do you have that fit with this business idea? Do you have experienced staff in this industry?

A description of the market for your product or service. Here, you should detail numbers in your market, why the market wants what you are going to sell, and include information on the competition and cost/price comparisons between competitors and your organization.

A marketing plan. How are you going to find out what your markets want and then give it to them? How are you going to let them know that you exist? How are you going to assure that they are happy and bring others back with them? Who are your target markets and who are your secondary markets? This is the place to tell readers.

A financial plan. Here is the place to make your spreadsheets sing. In this area you need at least the following financial displays:

- Sources and applications of cash and capital.
- An equipment list.
- A list of start-up costs.
- A pricing estimate.

- A break-even analysis
- Cash flow estimates by month for the first year, by the quarter for years two and three
- Projected income and expenses by month for the first year, by quarter for years two and three
- Notes of explanation of the assumptions used for each of the displays

Business plan goals and objectives with a time line. In this segment, you break out who will do what and when. You need goals and objectives. Remember: A *goal* is a statement of desired outcome. It may or may not be quantified or have a deadline. An *objective* has to include four things:

1. Support of the goal
2. A quantified outcome
3. A deadline
4. A person responsible for its achievement

Don't skip this step—remember that this is the key to being able to delegate the work!

An appendix (if needed). Most businesses, for-profit or not-for-profit, put way too much stuff in their appendix. In fact, *stuff* is exactly the right word: They stuff the appendix as full as they can to impress people with the overall weight of the plan. Avoid this temptation. Put as few appendixes in as you can, and then add a list of other backup documents that a reader might want to see, and where they can be obtained.

All of these components come together to provide you, your staff, your board, and any outside readers with a good understanding of what you plan to do, how you plan to do it, and the things that can go wrong. I am a great believer in business planning and, to help you even more, have included a complete example of a business plan in the remainder of this chapter and in Chapter 7, Business Plan Financial Projections.

C. A SAMPLE BUSINESS PLAN

Now let's look at a sample business plan. This plan was written to help you better understand the end product of your business-planning efforts. It is a compendium of real plans that I have helped not-for-profits write over the past 20 years. In fact, four agencies that I worked with in the same year all developed janitorial services, and their plans were merged into this one.

As you go through the plan, you will see comments from me in shaded boxes like this

> Comments will look like this.

one. These are here to make a certain point and to minimize the disruption in your reading of the plan. You can ignore them on your first read through the plan and then go back and read them, if you like, on a second pass.

Additionally, please remember that this business plan was written to demonstrate the most complex form of not-for-profit business start-up: a second for-profit corporation. *The vast majority of readers will not have to go this route* and will be able to house their business inside their existing corporation. I'll give you much more information on this in Chapter 10, Technicalities: Unrelated Business Income Tax and Corporate Structuring. But, even if you don't set up a for-profit, the plan's format is transferable to your business venture. The need to describe what you are doing, who you are doing it for, and how you are going to do it remains the same.

BACKGROUND OF THE NOT-FOR-PROFIT, INC. (NFP)

and Its Wholly Owned, For-Profit Subsidiary Corporation,
Enterprise Janitorial Services, Inc. (EJS)
The Organization Whose Business Plan Appears on the Following Pages

BACKGROUND INFORMATION

The Not-For-Profit (NFP) is a not-for-profit provider of vocational and residential services to over 150 persons annually in the town of Anywhere. The NFP has been in operation 36 years and has a $2.6 million annual budget that comes from the state and federal governments and private sources. In recent years, The NFP's funding has not been keeping pace with inflation. There are percentage increases in funding each year, but costs are rising at a greater rate. The NFP also has an ever increasing service demand that is difficult for the agency to meet.

The NFP's board of directors voted to begin and operate a business to provide jobs to the graduates of its vocational training program (who have disabilities) and to other people in the community, and to give the vocational services director a new challenge. The vocational services director has been with the NFP for five years and is a capable manager who is dedicated to the organization's cause. He is restless in his job and desires a higher salary and new incentives. As president and manager of Enterprise

Janitorial Services (EJS), he is eligible for profit-sharing and will have the opportunity to manage a business and face a great challenge in making this fledgling business a success. His ability to work well with disabled clients is a great asset since eight of the employees hired initially are graduates of the NFP's vocational program. The NFP also hopes that EJS will earn a profit. A certain percentage of that profit can be turned back to the NFP—as the owner of Enterprise Janitorial Services—on an annual basis in the form of dividends. These profits, if any, will be used for service expansion in the vocational services department and specialized vocational training.

Why did the NFP decide to operate a for-profit subsidiary corporation as opposed to running the business within its own 501(c)(3) corporation or operating it as another not-for-profit?

The NFP board of directors debated this point at length. After listing all the pros and cons, the directors chose a wholly owned, for-profit subsidiary. The following is a list of their reasons why.

1. As a for-profit corporation, EJS does not face the cries of unfair competition from the business community that often arise when a not-for-profit begins to compete with traditional businesses. As a for-profit corporation, EJS is taxed just as any other corporation would be.

2. A for-profit corporation can obtain capital more easily than a not-for-profit and many government loans and loan guarantee programs are only available to for-profits. In addition, banks and other lenders understand for-profits.

3. The NFP wants to make a substantial profit and also hire clients who graduate from the NFP's program and have difficulty finding immediate employment in the competitive employment market. EJS also wants to hire people with certain expertise, not necessarily related to the NFP, as the janitorial business expands.

4. The NFP's vocational services director is a dedicated employee but is looking for a new challenge. By making him EJS's president and manager, the NFP gives him a new opportunity that hopefully increases his salary and keeps him involved with the organization. As an added incentive, EJS has set up a profit-sharing program for him.

These reasons are the actual reasons that the not-for-profits used in developing their second corporations. The reader should note that numbers 3 and 4 can easily be accomplished within a not-for-profit structure.

Enterprise Janitorial Service, Inc.

A Subsidiary Corporation of the Not-For-Profit, Inc.

Business Plan

June ____

Enterprise Janitorial Service, Inc.

60 W. 53rd Street

Anywhere, USA 06560

(217) 444-5540

This business plan is the property of Enterprise Janitorial Service, Inc. (EJS). Because it contains confidential information proprietary to EJS, no copies may be made whatsoever of the contents herein nor any part thereof, nor should the contents be disclosed to any party not previously authorized to discuss said contents by EJS. This copy must be returned to EJS upon request.

Contents

> Remember to put page numbers in. They are not included here as the page numbers of the book and the page numbers of the plan would conflict.

I. THE SUMMARY

The Organization

The Enterprise Janitorial Service (EJS) is a subsidiary corporation of the Not-For-Profit (the NFP), a 36-year-old stable provider of vocational and residential services to over 150 residents of the Anywhere community. The NFP's $2.6 million budget comes from the state and federal government and private sources. (Income sources by percentage: 61 percent from the state and federal governments; 35 percent from other revenue such as client fees, investments, and sales and service; and 3.8 percent from public support such as the United Way, contributions, and fund-raising projects.) The NFP is establishing this fledgling corporation, Enterprise Janitorial Service, to provide employment to graduates of its vocational program and to other persons in the Anywhere community. The NFP also wants to earn added income for its programs and to compete fairly with other janitorial services of its type. This business plan is for a profit-making corporation.

The Service

EJS will be selling competitively priced, high-quality, dependable full-maintenance janitorial services to new and recently renovated large office building managers, tenants of such buildings, and small to medium-sized retail store managers, predominantly located on the west side of Anywhere. A full-time manager—formerly the vocational services director at the NFP, a part-time supervisor, and eight employees—all graduates of the NFP's vocational program—will make up the preliminary staffing of EJS. Each night two crews will work four to eight hours, depending on the workload, to clean contracted offices, stores, and office buildings twice a week. Contracts will be charged on a monthly basis at the rate of $0.15 per square foot.

> Look at the definition of the service. Then go down to the Marketing section and see what it was that the building services managers asked for. Is EJS giving its markets what they want?

The Markets

Business activity in Anywhere is growing. There are 25 new office buildings under construction on the west side of town and considerable renovation of office space in the downtown area. In addition, there are new residential developments on the west side of town and an influx of 92 retail stores moving in to take advantage of this growing market for goods. EJS has targeted new office buildings on the west side of town as its primary market. A secondary market is the group of west-side retailers since they have a consistent need for quality floor care services. EJS will also attempt to concentrate its business activity in the west side of town to eliminate travel time between jobs. No job, however, will be turned down unless it is more than 12 miles outside the Anywhere community.

The Marketing Plan

During the feasibility study, office building owners, office managers, retail store managers, and others who contracted for janitorial services were polled to find out what their service needs are. Repeatedly, the overwhelming response from 85 percent of those individuals polled was the need for a "high-quality, dependable service that is fairly priced." EJS's marketing strategy focuses on the quality and dependability issues and full-maintenance services in its advertising and promotion. Because the organization is using former clients, it is able to eliminate the turnover problems that most janitorial services experience and price its services fairly. EJS also emphasizes its relationship to the NFP, an organization that maintains a respected position in the community.

Financing Required

The Not-For-Profit is investing $20,000 in Enterprise Janitorial Services. The NFP corporation will own all 20,000 shares of EJS stock. EJS is requesting a $25,000 loan from the Small Business Administration at 9 percent over a five-year period. The NFP also agrees to lend EJS $10,000 for working capital. The $55,000 will be used to purchase two vans at a total cost of $24,000 and equipment at $7,175. The remaining $23,825 provides EJS with additional working capital.

> In less than two pages, you now know what the NFP is going to do, with whom, for whom, how, and with what financing.

II. THE NFP, ENTERPRISE JANITORIAL SERVICES, AND ITS BUSINESS

The Organization

The Not-For-Profit (NFP) has a history of providing high-quality residential and vocational training to the people of Anywhere. Since its founding 36 years ago, over 40,000 people have been served by the NFP's highly qualified 118 staff people and board members, all of whom are well-known community leaders in Anywhere.

While the NFP is funded by the state and federal governments and receives a substantial income from private sources, the cost of providing services continues to rise annually. To keep pace with the need for added dollars and an increased service demand, the NFP is planning to profitably operate Enterprise Janitorial Services as its subsidiary for-profit corporation.

The Service

Enterprise Janitorial Service will sell its janitorial services to new or recently renovated large office buildings and recently built small to medium-sized retail stores within the Anywhere community, predominantly on the west side of town. Other customers will be those building managers or office managers who have expressed dissatisfaction with their present janitorial service. EJS's service will be dependable, will pay close attention to detail, and will be very competitively priced. This janitorial service will provide total maintenance—floor cleaning and buffing, vacuuming, rug cleaning on a regular basis—as a part of the standard price, restroom cleaning, dusting, and the emptying of trash cans.

Six nights a week, two 4-person EJS crews will each clean for four to eight hours. Based on preliminary research, four people doing routine cleaning without heavy maintenance can clean a 2,000-square-foot office in about one-half hour. In a month's time, this office will require seven full hours of cleaning since full maintenance will be a part of the contract. EJS's target is to clean 55,000 square feet every two weeks by the third year. (EJS has signed one contract to immediately begin the cleaning of a 7,500-square-foot office building.)

The Target Market

The target markets for EJS are managers of new or recently renovated large office buildings which provide janitorial services as a part of the lease, tenants of large buildings that contract independently for janitorial services on the west side of town, and managers who are unhappy with their present janitorial services. Business activity in Anywhere is growing and new commercial construction is currently proceeding at a rapid rate. Many new office buildings are under construction or renovation on the west side of town and in the downtown area. These new buildings offer a ready market in the next 18 months or two years for enterprising providers of janitorial services. A secondary type of customer is small to medium-sized retailers on the west side of town that are in need of high-quality floor care services.

Potential Customer Reactions and Need for This Service

During its feasibility study of this venture, a representative sample of 20 retailers and 20 office managers was asked about present cleaning services. An overwhelming 85 percent of those polled responded that finding and retaining a dependable, high-quality janitorial service in Anywhere is very difficult. EJS plans to provide such good service that word of mouth will spread quickly and give the janitorial service many new opportunities. (EJS has already signed its first contract with a 7,500-square-foot office building on the west side.) Due to the great influx of people to the west side of town and the expanding commercial office space, both EJS's target markets are growing at a rapid pace and the need for janitorial services is a natural consequence.

The Sales Strategy

A record of telephone survey respondents was kept during the feasibility study. Those respondents who were in need of janitorial help will be added to EJS's list of target consumers which now includes the names of 40 potential customers. Other target consumers include managers of new or recently renovated large office buildings and retail outlets within Anywhere, predominantly on the west side of town. EJS will attempt to get contracts for entire buildings or contracts with most of the tenants within a building to avoid moving equipment from one building to another to cost-effectively maximize the allotted time each evening. Initial contact with these target consumers will be made by a sales representative who will telephone people included on the list of target customers. These people will also receive a promotional flyer. The flyer will be enclosed with a special letter written to each of the target consumers. An introductory price promotion will be offered to these organizations to entice them to give EJS's service a try. A coupon will entitle the user to have 20 percent of his or her square footage cleaned free of charge if he/she contracts with EJS's janitorial service between the months of September and December of this year. (EJS charges $0.15 a square foot per month for its service.) The one-time promotion is an attempt to get the customer to try the service and find out how reliable it is. Hopefully, this effort will lead to permanent work contracts.

In addition, a display ad will run in the yellow pages of the local telephone book and ads will also be placed in the Sunday edition business section of the newspaper on a periodic basis. The newspaper and other community information sources will be scanned daily to get information on new or recently renovated offices and retail stores opening within Anywhere and to get a feel for the activities of competing janitorial services. EJS will also monitor the granting of building permits within Anywhere to track commercial development that may lead to potential business.

III. THE MARKET DESCRIPTION

The Target Markets

The target markets of Enterprise Janitorial Services are as follows:

- New and recently renovated large office buildings that provide janitorial services as a part of the lease, predominantly those located on the west side of town
- Tenants within buildings that do not provide janitorial services
- New small to medium-sized retail stores that need quality floor care services, predominantly those located on the west side of town
- Large office buildings and small to medium-sized retail outlets on the west side of town that have not yet been completed, but will be ready for occupancy in the next few months

EJS will attempt to get contracts for entire office buildings, thus saving travel time and movement of equipment between jobs, and the time and expense of contracting with each individual tenant.

In addition, preliminary research shows that there are many office and building managers who are unhappy with their present janitorial services. These buildings will also be a part of the target markets.

Business activity in Anywhere is growing, especially in the service area. According to a survey recently conducted by the Anywhere Chamber of Commerce, just over 60 percent of the Anywhere employment opportunities are in the service area. This percentage is predicted to grow due to the influx of service industries moving into Anywhere and creating more offices. There are many new office buildings under construction on the west side of town and considerable renovation of office space in the downtown area. In addition, there are new residential developments on the west side of town and an influx of retail stores tapping this new market.

> As you have probably already noticed, there is some repetition in the plan. This is intentional. Key areas such as a description of the service, the target markets, and competition need to be discussed in several places for one reason: Many people who look at the plan won't read all of it. By putting the crucial information in a number of places, you assure that everyone sees it. And, for those who do read the entire plan, the repetition of the information assures that they will remember it.

The Competition

According to the State Employment Services (SES), there were 500 janitorial service jobs in the Anywhere area in the last quarter of last year. This represents approximately one-half of 1 percent of the total nonagricultural employment figures for Anywhere. These figures probably understate the total employment in building maintenance services because many janitorial jobs are performed by small firms which are not included in the monthly employment survey conducted by the SES. Service jobs, particularly business services jobs, represent one of the fastest-growing employment sectors both in the nation and in Anywhere. It seems likely that the number of janitorial service jobs in Anywhere shares in this recent expansion.

Based on the yellow pages of the telephone directory, there are 40 janitorial services listed in Anywhere. About five of these specialize in windows and three are residential only. The remaining 32 are general cleaning services specializing in commercial cleaning. Only two are nationally recognized franchise companies.

In the Anywhere area, janitorial services are provided to commercial users in a variety of ways. Some businesses own their own cleaning equipment and hire part-time employees to serve as janitors. Other businesses maintain verbal agreements with an outside person or cleaning service to provide both equipment and janitorial labor. Still other businesses maintain formal, written cleaning contracts with firms which provide both janitorial services and equipment. Most of these contracts contain clauses requiring 30 days written notice by either party desiring to terminate the agreement.

Over 85 percent of the office managers and retailers interviewed during the feasibility study stressed the need for dependability in a janitorial service. They emphasized that there is a major problem with poor quality and inattention to detail by their present cleaning service providers. Many of the problems that janitorial services have relate to high employee turnover and poor management.

EJS will be able to eliminate many of the problems in the reliability area since it has a pool of qualified laborers continually graduating from its vocational program upon which it can draw. At least two new employees will be trained at all times and will be on call in case of illness and vacations. Also, in comparison with other janitorial services, EJS is paying comparatively high salaries to its manager and supervisor to get qualified, reliable personnel who know how to manage.

Over 90 percent of the 40 people polled who contract for janitorial services said they like a full-maintenance service that does not charge extra for interior window cleaning, rug shampooing, or floor cleaning and waxing. EJS has set up its service to be a full-maintenance service. No extra charges will be made for these added services.

Price Comparisons

EJS will charge $0.15 a square foot per month for cleaning. EJS's cleaning service will include total maintenance of the commercial space two times a week. EJS will not only do basic cleaning, but rug shampooing as needed, interior window washing, and floor scrubbing and buffing on a regular basis.

The two nationally recognized, franchised janitorial services in Anywhere charge $0.15 a square foot per month for cleaning. This does not include full maintenance. These companies charge their customers extra for rug cleaning, interior window washing, floor scrubbing and buffing.

Other small firms in Anywhere charge $0.10 a square foot, but this, again, does not include full maintenance and most of them clean an office only once a week. The extra services previously listed must be scheduled separately and then added as extra charges. See the following table for a comparison of prices.

Price Comparisons

Nationally Franchised Janitorial Services	Most Small Services Locally Owned	Enterprise Janitorial Services, Inc.
$.15 a square foot per month	$.10 a square foot per month	$.15 a square foot per month
Two times a week service	Once a week service	Two times a week service
Not full maintenance	Not full maintenance	Full maintenance*

* *Full maintenance* means that rug cleaning, interior window washing, floor scrubbing and buffing are included in the regular monthly charge.

IV. THE MARKETING PLAN

The Markets

EJS targets large office buildings that provide janitorial services as a part of the lease, tenants of buildings without janitorial services, and small to medium-sized retail stores on the west side of Anywhere as its primary markets.

Large office buildings and small to medium-sized retail outlets that are newly constructed or that will be completed in the next few months are priorities since many of these buildings have not contracted for janitorial services.

Customers

Customers will be building superintendents, office managers, store managers, and other people who contract for janitorial services within the target markets.

Research was conducted by EJS's manager and a list of 40 names and addresses of potential customers was compiled by EJS based on its target markets. EJS's manager has arranged a contract with the management of a 7,500-square-foot office building. Ongoing efforts will be made to continue to ask and respond to the changing wants of our target markets.

Competitors

Based on the yellow pages of Anywhere's telephone directory, there are 40 janitorial services within the Anywhere area. About five of these specialize in windows and three are residential only. The remaining 32 are general cleaning services specializing in commercial cleaning. Only two of these competitors are nationally franchised companies.

The nationally franchised janitorial services charge $0.15 a square foot per month to clean two times a week. They do not provide full-maintenance services without an additional charge. Most small services that are locally owned charge $0.10 a square foot per month for once a week. This service is not full maintenance. EJS is charging $0.15 a square foot per month for cleaning service twice a week. This is for full-service maintenance.

The research conducted during the feasibility study shows that the competition is not doing the best job in meeting the needs of EJS's target customers. A sample of 40 people contracting for janitorial services was polled. Over 60 percent of the respondents said there was a major problem with poor quality and a lack of attention to detail by their present janitorial services. Ninety percent of the people polled said they want full-maintenance service that does not charge extra for interior window cleaning, rug shampooing, or floor cleaning and waxing. They also said they are willing to pay somewhat more per month to have these services included automatically.

> This section gives you a lot of data to consider. Remember that data and statistics are fine, but only if you provide two things. First, the source of the information. Where did it come from? Second, your interpretation of the information. What does it mean to you? This plan does both.

The Macroenvironment of the Business

There is a great influx of service businesses coming into the Anywhere area. According to a survey recently conducted by the Anywhere Chamber of Commerce, just over 60 percent of the Anywhere employment opportunities are in the service area.

The county planning commission figures show the following:

- The Anywhere unemployment rate is just under 7 percent.
- The average family income is $35,000 annually.
- Over 38 percent of the population have college degrees.
- Over 66 percent of the population graduated from high school.
- The primary source of household earnings comes from wages, salaries, and earnings.
- The present population statistic is at 650,000 and is predicted to grow by 12 percent through 2000.

According to the Anywhere Board of Realtors, most of the new housing construction is taking place on the west side of town. The same is true for commercial office and retail space. Construction starts for commercial office space are up 5 percent in comparison to last year.

A survey conducted by the United Way of Anywhere in 1995 shows the following information on Anywhere's population:

- Married couples account for approximately 70 percent of all households.
- The median age in Anywhere is 35 years old.
- The mean age is 40 years old.
- The percentage of new households started by married-couple families has increased by 40 percent since 1982–1983 and by 65 percent since 1987–1988.
- 90 percent of the population is white.
- 3 percent of the population is African-American.
- 5 percent of the population is Hispanic.
- 71 percent of the population is Protestant.
- 25 percent of the population is Catholic.
- 3 percent of the population is Jewish.
- Approximately 93 percent of the population is employed.

These statistics show that the Anywhere population is highly educated, primarily in their thirties and forties, and starting their families. This is a good sign for future growth and stability for the business community, especially the service industries. The Anywhere Chamber of Commerce predicts that this data attracts other service-type industries to Anywhere since there is a pool of well-educated, upwardly mobile individuals making up the workforce.

While the state's treasury is growing along with the population, there is a definite propensity to lower taxes and reduce government services. EJS's parent corporation, the Not-For-Profit, has not experienced any service reductions, but the rate of income increases for services has declined over the past two to three years. As a result, the NFP has a strong commitment to Enterprise Janitorial Services since some of the profits of EJS will come back to the Not-For-Profit in the form of after-tax dividends.

Due to the heavy influx of service industries which require office space and the continued increase in new office and retail building construction, EJS's market is ample, even with the current number of janitorial service competitors.

Potential Pitfalls

Established competition in the janitorial service field is a concern for this new corporation. Advance research shows that over 60 percent of the people polled are unhappy with their present cleaning service. This clearly means there is a need for an alternative service. It is EJS's role to fill in the gap. As with all new businesses, developing a reputation and credibility takes time. EJS allows for this building of business in its financial documentation. However, the success of EJS's marketing plan will determine its future profitability.

One problem that might affect EJS is the rapid expansion of business. The company is prepared to hire employees outside those being referred by the NFP. If this occurs, salaries for people being brought in from the general employment market will have to be higher than what is offered to those who are now starting with the company. This can cost EJS more than anticipated over a period of time.

The other problem with rapid expansion is quality control. EJS is making a strong commitment to quality janitorial services and strives to meet the standards it sets for itself, no matter what the circumstances. At some point, the growth of the company may have to be stalled if the workload becomes more than the company can handle.

Finally, EJS's relationship to the NFP can be a potential problem as well as an asset. In some cases, the hiring of former clients may be looked upon as a public service and encouraged. In other instances,

> To paraphrase the bumper sticker, "STUFF HAPPENS!" There will always be things that can go wrong, and by listing them, you show the reader how you plan to deal with them if they occur.

potential customers may have difficulty accepting the concept and will be concerned about the quality of the janitorial service. EJS will use national statistics that show that clients have a lower absentee rate than other employees and that their productivity is unusually high when compared to the norm.

EJS does not want to conceal its relationship to the NFP. The excellent reputation and track record of the NFP in Anywhere gives EJS stability. As the company grows and develops its own image and position in the community, the less EJS will have to rely on the NFP and its reputation.

V. THE FINANCIAL PLAN

The financial plan for EJS is provided in Chapter 7, Business Plan Financial Projections, along with a detailed discussion of how to develop your own financials.

VI. GOALS AND OBJECTIVES

Goal One: Prepare for opening of the business by (date).

> Objective 1-1.   Order needed supplies within 10 days of obtaining financing (EJS Director)
>
> Objective 1-2.   Select employees from vocational programs by (date) (EJS Director)
>
> Objective 1-3.   Hire supervisors by (date) (EJS Director)
>
> Objective 1-4.   Train new employees as necessary by (date) (EJS Director and supervisors)
>
> Objective 1-5.   Plan evening work and transport schedule by 10 days prior to opening of EJS (EJS Director)

Goal Two: Obtain needed financing

> Objective 2-1.   Obtain loan from NFP following board approval of plan (EJS Director)
>
> Objective 2-2.   Obtain NFP stock funds and set up EJS as separate for-profit by (date) (EJS Director)
>
> Objective 2-3.   With finance director and banker, apply for SBA loan within 10 days of board approval of business plan (EJS Director)

Goal Three: Market EJS to the target markets

> Objective 3-1.   Develop marketing materials within 15 days of board approval (EJS Director)
>
> Objective 3-2.   Develop contract agreement and bid sheet within 10 days of board approval (EJS Director)

Objective 3-3.   Make 15 cold calls per week to get two customers a week for eight weeks prior to EJS opening (EJS Director)

Objective 3-4.   Mail out 500 letters of introduction and marketing materials within 30 days of board approval (EJS Director)

Goal Four: Maintain quality and customer satisfaction

Objective 4-1.   Survey five customers by phone or e-mail weekly to assure satisfaction with services (EJS Director)

Objective 4-2.   Develop and administer annual written survey of customers to assure satisfaction and to ask for ways to improve services. Accomplish this within 12 months of opening (EJS Director)

Objective 4-3.   Provide customer service training to all employees at least three hours per year and refresher training in janitorial techniques at least two hours per year (EJS Director)

Goal Five: Expand EJS to maximize profits and mission return

Objective 5-1.   Attain an average of 21,500 feet per month cleaned within two months of opening (EJS Director)

Objective 5-2.   Attain an average of 33,500 feet per week cleaned within four months of opening (EJS Director)

Objective 5-3.   Attain an average of 55,000 feet per week cleaned within seven months of opening (EJS Director)

Objective 5-4.   Attain an average of 80,000 feet per week cleaned within 12 months of opening (EJS Director)

Objective 5-5.   Report financial condition of EJS monthly to NFP board (EJS Director)

VII. THE APPENDIX

Put a *minimum* of items in your appendix—the more you put, the less likely people are to read it. Have a list of appendixes available for review, but don't give everything to everybody.

Things that *might* be appropriate to include in the EJS appendix:

Resume of president and manager of Enterprise Janitorial Services (formerly the vocational services director of the NFP)

Resume of the part-time supervisor

Letter from a contracted customer, or customer contract

A completed financial estimate

Credit information

The Not-For-Profit annual report

In the next chapter, we'll look at the financials for the EJS business plan, as well as give you some hands-on suggestions on how to develop your own financials with as little pain and strain as possible.

Note that the EJS plan was not long, even if you add 7 to 10 pages for financials. You don't need to kill a lot of trees to write a great plan. Remember, *quality*, not *quantity*, is what you are trying for.

RECAP

In this chapter, we looked at the business plan, its development, and why it is important. I first told you why it is so crucial to complete the risk-reduction process and write your plan. The three reasons I gave were as follows:

1. Writing a business plan forces you to take an objective, critical, unemotional look at your business project in its entirety.
2. The finished product is an operating tool that, if properly used, will help you manage your business and work toward its success.
3. The completed business plan is your means of communicating your ideas to others and provides the basis for your financing proposal.

We then turned to the contents of the business plan. To review, these were the following:

A title page

A table of contents

A summary of the plan

A description of your organization and its business

A description of the market for your product or service

The marketing plan

Financial projections

Goals and objectives with a time line

An appendix, if needed

Then, I showed you a sample business plan for Enterprise Janitorial Services. This plan not only showed you an example, it also provides the basis for our discussion in the next chapter on how to develop your financials. Let's get on to that now.

QUESTIONS FOR DISCUSSION: CHAPTER 6

1. How do we best get the business plan completed? Who should head up the task?

2. What information from the feasibility study can we use as it now is, and what do we need to update or expand?

3. What is our intended audience? Do we think at this point we'll need to go for outside financing? Will we need to show the finished plan to our bank, our main funder, or anyone else? Should we run it by them even if we don't have to?

7

Business Plan Financial Projections

OVERVIEW

In this chapter you will learn about the following:

- ➤ Getting the Numbers Right
- ➤ Developing Your Projections
- ➤ Sample Financials for Enterprise Janitorial Services

Now we get down to the nitty-gritty, the financial projections. While mission is always foremost, you still have to run the numbers to see what the money side will look like after you begin your new venture, expand a current service, move into a new market, or start serving a new population. In this chapter, we'll look at some overall rules and suggestions for developing your financial projections. I'll provide you with some templates that you can use (and that you will have a chance to put into use in Chapter 8, Applying the Lessons: A Step-by-Step Business-Planning Exercise), and then we'll look at the financials that accompany the business plan for Enterprise Janitorial Services that you read in Chapter 6, The Business Plan.

By the end of this chapter, you should have a working understanding of the why and the how regarding your business development numbers. As a social entrepreneur, you are trying to take *reasonable* risk on behalf of the people that you serve. Developing good, accurate, readable financials will help you, your staff, and your board immensely as you try to keep the risks reasonable.

A. GETTING THE NUMBERS RIGHT

Okay, first some bad news: Your financial projections are, at best, educated guesses, no more, no less. You are putting down numbers that correspond to your best guess as to what will happen three, six, nine, 12, even 36 months out into the future. There is even an accounting term for this: *pro forma*, which just means "projected." Why is this bad news? Because you are betting real money on the validity of your projections, sometimes a whole lot of money. And pretty soon your business plan projections will require a go/no-go decision from your management team and board of directors. Then, it's for real. This is what is known as the leap off the entrepreneurial cliff. The question is, how solid are the assumptions upon which you have built your projections? The better they are, the more educated your guesses are, the shorter the cliff you are jumping off, and the softer the landing you may make. The more wild, unresearched, or unchecked your financials are, the taller the cliff and the sharper the rocks at the bottom.

In Chapter 6, The Business Plan, I told you that it was crucial that the marketing, sales, and other information that you put in your plan be accurate, sourced, and analyzed. That was all true, and now those marketing and sales assumptions get put into dollars and cents. So, what you are doing at this point is translating your best information (some would say best guesses) on marketing, sales, customer wants, and methods of meeting those wants into cash flow, income and expense, start-up cost, and sources and applications of funds. It is important to remember this connection and, unfortunately, too many people do not. If your sales projections are not in line with your income numbers, or your marketing ideas do not show up in your expenses, the plan simply will not work. Those who review it will find it disjointed and inconsistent, and will probably not approve your project.

In addition, it is important to get numbers as accurate as possible because minor errors from inaccuracy or rounding have a bad habit of multiplying into big ones. For instance, if you underestimate your personnel expenses (including fringes) for your project by just 1 percent, and overestimate your income by just 1 percent, all of a sudden you are about 1.8 percent off (since personnel consumes approximately 80 percent of most not-for-profit expenditures). Although 1.8 percent may not seem like much, if the venture is projected to bring in, say, $400,000 per year, the error becomes $7,200, not an insignificant sum. Even if the venture is much smaller, that 1.8 percent error might be the difference between your board going ahead (thinking the idea would make some money) and not. So, run the numbers thoroughly, and try not to balance rounding too little, and perhaps spending too much time on the details, and rounding too much, and having the overall projections be significantly off.

Now that we've agreed that accuracy is both important and worth the effort, let's look at some ways to keep those numbers both accurate and in synch with the rest of the plan.

1. Use an Electronic Spreadsheet

The development of financials is not a one-shot task. You will gather information, make initial estimates of price, costs, markets, and so forth, and then constantly refine them. This is what electronic spreadsheets such as Excel and Lotus 1-2-3 were designed for. They make your task manageable. If you have them already, fine; use them. If you don't, get them and learn how to use them. And, if you have someone internally that is a spreadsheet expert, consult that person on how to best set up the templates for this purpose.

☞ **HANDS ON:** One of the real benefits—and dangers—of electronic spreadsheets is that you can link cells in the sheet, so that if you change a number in one cell, it results in a change in one or more linked cells. This makes revisions really easy, but also can present a danger if you assume certain things are linked and they are not. For example, if a portion of your fixed costs, such as rent, goes up, have you linked the spreadsheet to show an increase in both costs (in the income and expense statement) and disbursements (in the cash flow)? This is all the more reason to use a spreadsheet expert.

2. Consult Your Financial Manager

You have a financial manager, and he or she needs to be in on the development of the business plan and financials. No, the financial manager doesn't need to *do* the financials, but he or she should help in their development. You see, this person will know where costs really are hidden. He or she can help you with estimates of cost increases. But both you and the financial manager need to learn how to develop business financials, as they are almost certainly different than the financials you currently use for your not-for-profit services. Have the financial manager help, but don't let him or her do all the work.

3. Include *All* Your Costs

This is the biggest single mistake I see, and I see it all the time. Organization after organization comes to me with a plan that doesn't include rent, or part of the executive director's time, or a line for insurance. Why? "Because our grant already covers that." This is the most common answer. Don't fall victim to this bad habit of cost shifting. If you are going to make an accurate assessment of risk, put all the costs in, and let the idea stand or fall on its own. Again, here, consult your financial manager, as that person knows what costs have already been shifted in or out of your budget.

4. Have an Outside Reviewer

The second most common mistake I see is an organization that has not had someone from the outside check its financials. This lack of an objective outside viewpoint leads to financials in which there is a debt shown on the balance sheet but no debt service on the cash flow or interest expense on the profit and loss statement. These kind of problems are understandable as your financials will go through many, many versions before you finish them, but an outside check by a business consultant, banker, or accountant will help find errors early.

Now that you have heard my admonitions, let's turn to actually putting together your financial projections.

B. DEVELOPING YOUR PROJECTIONS

It is time to look at the sequence of work that you should do to develop your financial projections. There are three main steps in the process, the first being to *gather your financial data.*

In the early stages of product or service selection and feasibility analysis, you gathered most of the information you now need to prepare your business plan. Your work at this stage is to refine and organize that information, to check the accuracy of your estimates, and to replace as many estimates as you can with firm figures. For example, for the purpose of your feasibility study, you may estimate that your rent payment is $600 per month. In your actual business plan, you may state that you are leasing property at 1124 East Church Street for $635 dollars per month.

The following is a description and listing of the information you need for your business plan, and there are forms that you will be using in Chapter 8, Applying the Lessons: A Step-by-Step Business-Planning Exercise, to actually complete a business plan.

1. Sales Target for the First Three Years

In order to make reasonable financial projections, you need to predict as accurately as possible what your volume of business will be. There are two major constraints here: the market and the assets—such as money, skill, and time—that can be put into the enterprise. One way to approach these constraints is to estimate, based on your market research, what the potential market for your product or service is if you have no money, skills, or time restraints. The next factor is your internal constraints. This information allows you to estimate with some confidence what your potential sales will be. You should project sales for at least a three-year period.

Be careful not to project growth that cannot be sustained by your cash flow or by your markets. For example, if you are selling janitorial services in a community of 10,000 people with only 25 business establishments, there is only a limited number of the businesses that may be willing to buy your services. This is true even if you provide top-quality service and beat the price of all the competition. You simply cannot sell everyone. Conversely, in a big city, there could be a nearly unlimited market for janitorial service at the quality and price you offer. But if your potential workforce is limited to about 10 employees, it would be impossible for you to reach your entire potential market. (See Exhibit 7-1.)

2. Pricing Information

Pricing is the art of finding the price that your market will pay that will cover your production costs and provide a reasonable return on your investment. By using the information you gathered in your marketing research, you can determine the going price or price range for products or services that are similar to yours (see Exhibit 7-2). Next, set a target for the amount of profit you wish to make during the first three years of operation. This information is used to set the price after you analyze the various costs involved in your operation. You may well need to modify this price a number of times, but you need to have a starting target price.

Price is made up of three parts:

1. Fixed costs
2. Variable costs
3. Profits

Each of these tend to make the price go higher. What holds price down is competition, or the *market*. There are two major problems people have when defining price. The first is that they assume that lower is always better. It's *not*. Remember this: It is *never* about price. It is *always* about value. What value do you provide in your service or product that would make someone want to pay your price?

Second, people make some technical mistakes in assessing their fixed costs. They do one of these three things:

1. Not including *all* the costs—we've already covered that.
2. Assuming an optimistic (or pessimistic) sales forecast, which is why your sales projections are so important.
3. Having a fixed percentage administrative charge in the fixed costs. While this is easy and consistent, it always is wrong, and when you

Exhibit 7-1   Initial size of business form.

Initial Size of Our Business			
	Year One	**Year Two**	**Year Three**
Sales (in units of sale)			
Sales (in dollars)			

Rationale: *The reason we think we need to be this size to start.*

Checklist: *Will our market support this size? Can we produce this much product or service? Can we do it with a high level of quality and customer satisfaction?*

Exhibit 7-2   Pricing chart.

Item	Cost	Instructions
Fixed Costs per Year		
Units of Sales per Year		
Fixed Cost per Unit		Divide the Fixed Costs per Year by the Units of Sales per Year to arrive at Fixed Cost per Unit.
Variable Cost per Unit		
Profit per Unit		
Total Price per Unit		Add up the per unit costs to get the total price per unit.

are adding this amount into your fixed costs, it winds up with an inaccurate price.

In Chapter 8, Applying the Lessons: A Step-by-Step Business-Planning Exercise, I will also show you how to price for multiple items.

3. Start-up Costs
Start-up costs are the costs that you incur before the business opens up.

Capital items. These are the one-time purchase items that you need to operate your business. This category includes the purchase of land, buildings, equipment, and furniture. These are the assets that continue to benefit your business operation. Items such as inventory or supplies that are used in the course of conducting business are expenses. With the exception of land, you depreciate your capital assets. Depreciation is simply an accounting method of distributing capital costs to the expense of the business operation. Large-ticket items should routinely be depreciated even if the business is a not-for-profit; otherwise, you never recover your full costs.

☞ **HANDS ON:** For your larger expenses, review one or two financing options even if you plan at this point to pay cash. Borrowing or leasing might be more advantageous and you need this information to test the financing options.

Other initial costs. In addition to capital items, you have other costs related to getting your business started which are not reflected in your operating expenses. Items such as legal fees, costs incurred to set up an accounting system, licenses, and introductory advertising are included in this section. (See Exhibit 7-3.)

4. Operating Expenses
Fixed costs. These are the expenses that you pay whether or not you sell any product or service. They are sometimes called indirect costs or overhead. These expenses include such items as rent, heat and electricity, and salaries. Most of your fixed or indirect costs change at different levels of sales or production. For example, if you operate a mail-order nursery, you produce a certain limited number of plants to sell from one greenhouse. If you wish to sell more, you need two greenhouses. This action increases your capital costs and fixed costs. If you anticipate growth during the first three years of operation, you need to estimate your fixed costs at various sales levels and identify the levels where your fixed and capital costs increase.

Exhibit 7-3   Start-up cost estimation.

Start-up Cost Estimation	
Cost Item	Cost Estimate
Wages	
Benefits	
Training	
Rent	
Utilities	
Equipment (detail)	
Supplies (detail)	
Licenses	
Marketing (detail)	
Printing	
Travel	
Raw materials	
Engineering	
Legal	
Accounting	
TOTAL START-UP COSTS	

Variable costs. These are expenses that vary directly with the number of items or services you sell. Variable costs are also called direct costs. These costs depend on the type of business. If you manufacture a product, then all of the material costs are considered variable costs. If your product is made by workers who are paid only for contracted work, then their wages are part of the variable costs. If, however, your workers are salaried, you must pay them whether or not there is work to do. This makes salary expense a fixed cost.

The second step is to *analyze the financial data you have gathered.* After you organize the critical financial data, you are in a position to analyze the information to help you make decisions about financing and pricing your product or service. Examples of worksheets completed by Enterprise Janitorial Services are shown later.

5. Start-up Costs and Working Capital Needs

This section is a summary of all of the costs you must cover to start the business and keep it in operation until it becomes profitable. Look at the information you gathered in the previous section and place it in a spreadsheet that shows where your cash is being spent (such as for equipment, supplies, salaries, etc.) and when cash is coming in (loans, earned income, etc.). Exhibit 7-4 shows an example of such a spreadsheet. Do this by month, and then you will see how much cash you need to have access to in order to not go out of business while you are still in the start-up phase. EJS added in a three-month period of start-up costs after opening (which is relatively short) because the business already has fairly secure commitments for work. This means that income generates as soon as the business begins. When there is less certainty, it is wise to plan for a longer period of time without income.

The purpose of identifying your start-up costs is to uncover your financing needs. For example, later in the chapter, you will see that EJS's total start-up costs are $66,719. After doing a cash flow analysis, EJS determined that an initial investment of $55,000 is sufficient. Out of a total investment of $55,000, $31,175 is used to purchase equipment, while the remaining $23,825 is working capital.

6. Break-Even Analysis

Break-even analysis provides you with a sales objective that is expressed in either the number of dollars or units of production at which your business is neither making a profit nor losing money. The break-even point is the point where sales income is equal to fixed costs plus variable costs for a certain period of time. Break-even analysis is a technique used to analyze your cost information. The technique helps you to decide how much you

Exhibit 7-4   Working capital.

Working Capital Needs—Year One		
Item	**Item Need**	**Total Needs**
Projected Income		
Days to Payment		
Total Working Capital Needed (Income × (Days to Payment/365))	**(Copy Sum →)**	

Additional Cash Needs—Year One		
Equipment Purchases		
Minus Loans	( )	
Start-up Costs		
Total Additional Cash Needs	**(Copy Sum →)**	
Total Cash Needed—Year One		

have to charge at various levels of sales, how much you have to sell at various prices in order to get a return equal to your expenses, or whether you will have to wait forever to have enough income to cover your expenses.

The formula for breakeven is pretty simple. It is shown as follows:

Break-even volume = Fixed Cost / (Price − Variable Cost per Item)

You may find that to charge a competitive price, you have to produce an unrealistic number of sales to achieve a profit. In this case, you need to reexamine your cost assumptions to see whether expenses can be reduced. Alternately, you may find that your sales projections show that you won't even reach a break-even volume for three years. . . . Can you wait that long?

7. Pro Forma Profit and Loss Statement

This statement is a projection of your income and expenses. Like the break-even analysis, it provides a further check on the soundness of your venture. Most business plans project income and expense statements for at least three years. Experts recommend that you project income and expenses for a five-year period. However, the further you move from present day, the less meaningful your numbers become. To develop your profit and loss statement, simply use the figures from your operating expenses form for fixed expenses. Subtract your expenses from your income to show your pretax profit, add taxes if you anticipate incorporating your business as a for-profit enterprise, and subtract any profit sharing or bonuses. The final figure is your retained earnings or fund balance. Be sure to take a look at the pro forma profit and loss form discussion later in the chapter.

8. Pro Forma Cash Flow Analysis

Your cash flow is the most important analysis for internal management of your business. It is the document that banks are most interested in because it indicates your ability to pay back your debt. The cash flow analysis shows how much cash is needed, when it is needed, and where it comes from. After you develop the cash flow analysis, use it as a check on how your business is doing. If you spend more or take in less cash than you anticipate, you may run into trouble. Variation from your cash flow projection helps you see early on if you are likely to run into cash problems. This analysis gives you a chance to take action and correct the flow of cash before you run into serious shortage problems. Again, there is more about cash flow in a few pages.

Your next step is to *prepare the financial data to incorporate it into your formal business plan*. The financial section of your business plan should include the following displays.

- *Pro forma sources and applications of funds.* This statement identifies where you intend to secure the funds you need to begin your business and how you intend to spend the money. An example of a pro forma sources and applications of funds statement is included in the sample EJS business plan. In order to prepare this document, you must first look at your start-up costs and cash flow analysis to determine how much money you need to start the operation and how much working capital you need to carry the business until it generates its own revenue. Next, identify where you anticipate getting your money (your fund sources) in one column. In the second column, list the ways you intend to spend or apply the resources that are available.

- *The financial condition of the organization.* Be sure you include descriptive statements about the financial condition of the organization initiating the new business in this section of your business plan. This includes any information you believe reassures the bank that the financial position of the parent not-for-profit organization is sound. It should include your financial statements for at least three years as well as a current balance sheet. *Note:* You only need to do this if you are going outside for financing. If all of your financing will be internal, you don't need this display.

- *Pro forma balance sheet and profit and loss statements.* This statement is prepared to show the anticipated financial condition of your business to bankers and others who wish to help you finance your venture. I strongly suggest that the first year be month by month, and the second two years presented quarter by quarter. The first balance sheet shows where the business is on the first day of business, and the second, a year later.

- *Break-even analysis.* Include a short section that indicates the number of units you must sell at your current asking price in order to break even. If you can find any information about the business you are entering that indicates typical sales for your demography or any other information that shows costs and anticipated sales based on sound information, be sure to include it.

- *Pro forma cash flow.* Include a pro forma cash flow projection for at least three years. The first year is a month-by-month projection. The following years can be done on a quarterly basis. Remember, this is the most important document for your banker, and for you and your board of directors. Compile the information with care because it provides you with an invaluable measure of how your business will affect the rest of your organization.

C. SAMPLE FINANCIALS FOR ENTERPRISE JANITORIAL SERVICES

Now we can turn from the theoretical to the practical, with a review of Enterprise Janitorial Services' financials.

Financial Objectives

As shown in Exhibit 7-5 Enterprise Janitorial Services (EJS) is seeking a loan of $25,000 to purchase equipment, while maintaining sufficient cash reserves and working capital to successfully initiate a janitorial cleaning service. This sum, together with $20,000 in equity investment of the Not-For-Profit, will be sufficient to finance the business through the start-up phase so it can operate as a profitable enterprise.

Financial Condition of Owner

The Not-For-Profit, Inc. (the NFP) is the sole owner of Enterprise Janitorial Services, Inc. The NFP receives 3.8 percent of its funding from charitable sources, 61 percent from governmental sources and 35 percent from earned income. The NFP is spinning off Enterprise Janitorial Services (EJS) as a for-profit corporation to create jobs for former clients and others in the community as well as to earn additional income for the NFP. NFP's finances are shown in Exhibits 7-6 and 7-7.

The Board of the NFP in its February 12, _____ meeting approved the incorporation of EJS as a wholly owned subsidiary. It also approved an equity investment of $20,000 in the new corporation and a $10,000 working capital loan.

In addition to providing EJS with financial resources, The NFP will provide EJS with accounting services, an office, and storage space. EJS's

Exhibit 7-5   Enterprise Janitorial Services sources and applications of funding.

Sources		Applications	
Owner investment	$20,000	Purchase vans	$24,000
Small Business Administration loan 9% for 5 years	$25,000	Purchase equipment	$ 7,175
Working capital loan from the Not-for-Profit, Inc. 9% for 7 years	$10,000	Working capital	$23,825
TOTAL	$55,000	TOTAL	$55,000

Exhibit 7-6   The Not-For-Profit income and expense statements for years 1999–2001.

	1999	2000	2001
SUPPORT AND REVENUE			
Public Support:			
United Way	$45,876	$43,582	$40,000
Other Contributions	23,002	21,700	35,000
Designated Gifts	10,551	560	60
Fund-Raiser	18,967	18,019	3,000
TOTAL Public Support	**$98,396**	**$83,861**	**$78,060**
Government Revenue			
State Grant-In-Aid	967,990	967,067	980,000
Federal Title XX	241,118	265,230	254,621
Federal Title XIX	366,765	385,103	369,699
TOTAL Government Support	**$1,575,873**	**$1,617,400**	**$1,604,320**
Other Revenue			
Client Fees	251,986	229,765	199,876
Sales and Service	545,678	400,876	210,234
Income from Investments	112,876	95,678	91,851
Other Income	48	2,000	567
TOTAL SUPPORT AND REVENUE	**$2,584,857**	**$2,429,580**	**$2,184,908**
EXPENSES			
Salaries and Wages	1,416,000	1,359,360	1,200,897
Employee Benefits	266,560	215,232	180,135
Insurance	29,768	28,280	20,000
Interest	12,055	11,452	9,876
Outside Consulting	55,030	40,000	38,400
Rent	266,190	260,866	255,649
Food	120,876	114,832	110,239
Depreciation	92,114	82,903	79,586
Maintenance and Supplies	51,234	45,086	40,000
Miscellaneous	5,689	5,405	3,009
Staff Training	19,876	18,882	16,987
Staff Travel	16,543	15,716	14,000
Repairs	16,479	20,000	12,000
Building Maintenance	25,366	24,351	23,377
TOTAL EXPENSES	**$2,393,780**	**$2,242,365**	**$2,004,155**
EXCESS OF REVENUES OVER EXPENSES	**$191,077**	**$187,215**	**$180,753**
Fund Balance—START	$1,233,870	$1,046,655	$865,902
Fund Balance—END	$1,424,947	$1,233,870	$1,046,655

accounting and bookkeeping units will be kept completely separate from the NFP. Because the NFP has extra computer and clerical capacity it will provide these services to EJS at a much lower cost than if EJS hired its own bookkeeper. Fees for accounting services are based on the NFP staff time at cost. Rental and utility charges are based on the percent of the NFP building used by EJS. The NFP's overhead costs are equal to $5 per square foot. The records will be maintained according to generally accepted accounting practices and audited on a yearly basis.

Exhibit 7-7 The Not-For-Profit balance sheet, June 30.

	UN-RESTRICTED	RESTRICTED	ENDOWMENT FUND	TOTALS
Assets				
Current Assets				
Cash	$1,521	$523	$327	$2,371
Short-Term Securities	58,990	64,567	153,425	276,982
Accounts Receivable	94,789			94,789
Prepaid Expenses	1,425			1,425
Supplies	965			965
TOTAL Current Assets	157,690	65,090	153,752	376,532
Land, building, and equipment net of depreciation	1,655,678			1,655,678
Other Assets				
Long-Term Investments	367,432			367,432
Deferred Charges	5,000			5,000
TOTAL Other Assets	372,432	0	0	372,432
TOTAL Assets	$2,185,800	$65,090	$153,752	$2,404,642
Liabilities and Fund Balances				
Current Liabilities				
Accounts Payable	134,563			134,563
Accrued Expenses	99,654			99,654
Current Portion of Long-Term Debt	43,871			43,871
TOTAL Current Liab.	$278,088	0	0	278,088
Long-Term Debt	175,484			175,484
Deferred Revenue	10,765			10,765
Total Liabilities	$464,337	0	0	$464,337
Fund Balances	$1,721,463	$65,090	$153,752	$1,940,305
Total Liabilities and Fund Balances	$2,185,800	$65,090	$153,752	$2,404,642

Also shown are EJS's start-up costs (Exhibit 7-8), cash flow projection (Exhibit 7-9), and profit and loss projection (Exhibit 7-10).

NOTES TO THE FINANCIALS

Break-Even Analysis

Break-even analysis shows that at the price of $0.15 per square foot per month, EJS must clean a cumulative 584,148 square feet or average 48,679 square feet a month to break even. EJS anticipates it will reach this volume of sales within six months and will begin making a profit after that point.

Explanation for Income Projections

1. Gross sales are based on the estimated square footage of contracts. EJS charges $0.15 per square foot per month. In the first year, EJS

Exhibit 7-8   Start-up costs.

Capital equipment		
Two vans (used)		**$24,000**
Major cleaning equipment		**9,800**
4 vacuum cleaners	$ 1,300	
2 wet/dry tanks	2,000	
2 buffers	3,000	
1 wet extraction carpet cleaner	3,500	
General cleaning equipment		**1,950**
10 buckets	450	
10 wringers	700	
3 mop bucket dollies	240	
4 "wet floor" signs	60	
3 utility carts	500	
Other initial requirements		
License: City and county		**100**
Telephone: Installation		**425**
Office supplies and equipment		**750**
Chair	300	
Filing cabinet	200	
Desk	150	
Stationery	50	
Billing materials	60	
Introductory advertising		**2,910**
Brochure	1,500	
Postage	220	
Advertisements on van	300	
Business cards	50	
Contractual services (sales representative for 12 hours)	840	
Initial insurance		**8,700**
Prepaid liability insurance	8,000	
Van insurance (6 months prepaid)	700	
Three months operating expenses		**20,911**
Salaries		
1 manager/supervisor	3,750	
Part- time supervisor	1,374	
Hourly wages for workers	7,716	
Fringe benefits	2,054	
Materials and supplies	450	
Loan payment	1,036	
Interest	74	
Vehicle operation and maintenance	500	
Telephone	120	
Bookkeeping	75	
Advertising	375	
Depreciation	2,525	
Rent	712	
Repairs	150	
TOTAL START-UP COSTS		**$69,546**

Exhibit 7-9   Enterprise Janitorial Services pro forma cash flow analysis for year one.

MONTH	1	2	3	4	5	6	7	8	9	10	11	12	TTL
CONTRACTS IN SQ.FT.	7,500	21,500	29,500	33,500	37,500	47,500	55,000	55,000	55,000	55,000	55,000	55,000	
CASH RECEIPTS	1,125	3,225	4,425	5,025	5,625	7,125	8,250	8,250	8,250	8,250	8,250	8,250	76,050
DISBURSEMENTS													
Variable Labor	352	1,008	1,384	1,571	1,759	2,228	2,580	2,580	2,580	2,580	2,580	2,580	23,782
Variable Payroll/Fringe	56	161	221	251	281	356	413	413	413	413	413	413	3,804
Supplies	20	58	80	90	101	128	149	149	149	149	149	149	1,371
Advertising	2,200	430	150	150	150	150	150	150	150	150	150	150	4,130
Vehicle Operation	23	65	89	101	113	143	165	165	165	165	165	165	1,524
Repairs	7	19	27	30	34	43	50	50	50	50	50	50	460
Insurance	8,700	0	0	0	0	0	700	0	0	0	0	0	9,400
Legal & Accounting	500	27	27	27	27	27	27	27	27	27	27	27	797
Salaries	1,975	1,975	1,975	1,975	1,975	1,975	1,975	1,975	1,975	1,975	1,975	1,975	23,700
Loan 1	75	75	75	75	75	75	75	75	75	75	75	75	900
Loan 2	519	519	519	519	519	519	519	519	519	519	519	519	6,228
Telephone	40	40	40	40	40	40	40	40	40	40	40	40	480
Rent/Utilities	237	237	237	237	237	237	237	237	237	237	237	237	2,844
TOTAL DISBURSEMENTS	14,704	4,614	4,824	5,066	5,311	5,921	7,080	6,380	6,380	6,380	6,380	6,380	
NET CASH FLOW	(13,579)	(1,389)	(399)	(41)	314	1,204	1,170	1,870	1,870	1,870	1,870	1,870	
CUMULATIVE CASH FLOW	(13,579)	(14,968)	(15,367)	(15,408)	(15,094)	(13,890)	(12,720)	(10,850)	(8,980)	(7,110)	(5,240)	(3,370)	
STARTING CASH ON HAND	21,475	7,896	6,507	6,108	6,067	6,381	7,585	8,755	10,625	12,495	14,365	16,235	
CASH RECEIPTS	1,125	3,225	4,425	5,025	5,625	7,125	8,250	8,250	8,250	8,250	8,250	8,250	
CASH DISBURSEMENTS	14,704	4,614	4,824	5,066	5,311	5,921	7,080	6,380	6,380	6,380	6,380	6,380	
ENDING CASH ON HAND	7,896	6,507	6,108	6,067	6,381	7,585	8,755	10,625	12,495	14,365	16,235	18,105	

Exhibit 7-10   Enterprise Janitorial Services pro forma profit and loss statement three-year summary.

	YEAR 1	YEAR 2	YEAR 3
GROSS SALES	$ 76,050	$ 147,600	$ 198,000
OPERATING EXPENSES			
Salaries	20,500	25,000	30,000
Variable Labor	23,778	49,200	72,600
Fringe Benefits and Payroll Taxes	7,084	11,872	16,416
Materials and Supplies	1,369	2,657	3,564
Telephone	480	500	550
Legal/Accounting	800	1,000	1,500
Advertising	1,500	2,000	2,200
Rent/Utilities	2,848	2,848	2,848
Depreciation	9,025	9,025	9,025
Insurance	9,400	10,000	11,000
Licenses	100	100	100
Repairs	456	984	1,320
Vehicle Operation and Maintenance	1,521	2,952	3,960
Interest	2,982	2,982	2,982
TOTAL OPERATING EXPENSES	81,843	121,120	158,065
NET PROFIT(LOSS) PRETAX	(5,793)	26,480	39,935
TAXES	0	3,103	5,990
PROFIT SHARING	0	530	799
AFTER-TAX EARNINGS	(5,793)	22,847	33,146
EARNINGS TO DATE	$(5,793)	$17,054	$50,200

estimates that the maximum square feet contracted per month will be 55,000 square feet. This assumption is based on the marketing analysis. The pricing decision is based on a comparison with competitors. During the second year, 82,000 square feet of contracts are forecast and in year three, the square footage increases to 110,000. Even in year three, two teams of four, working eight hours a day can provide the required services. If square footage increases beyond 110,000 square feet, EJS must add an additional team and acquire new capital equipment.

2. Salaries are projected to increase over a three-year period. In addition, the part-time supervisor will be three-fourths-time in year two and full-time in year three.

3. Variable costs are estimated based on the number of square feet being cleaned twice a week. The following costs estimates are determined:

Variable Expense	Per Square Foot Costs
Workers wages	$0.0469
Payroll taxes	0.0075
Supplies/material	0.0027
Vehicle operation and maintenance	0.0030
Repairs	0.0009
Total Variable Costs	$0.0610

4. Legal/accounting includes accounting and bookkeeping services EJS will purchase from the NFP. Legal services were purchased by the NFP prior to the creation of EJS.

5. Advertising includes local newspaper ads and direct mail flyers. Major initial advertising expenses itemized in the Start-up Costs are not included here because they are not continuing operating costs.

6. Rent/utilities are purchased from the NFP for $5 per square foot. EJS's space needs are limited to 570 square feet since the only space needed is for storage and making appointments.

7. Depreciation is calculated for capital equipment, including the two used vans and major cleaning equipment. Depreciation is calculated on a three-year basis.

8. Insurance expense includes liability insurance for the organization.

9. Licenses include both city and state operating licenses.

10. Interest includes the interest due on both the SBA and the NFP loans.

11. Since EJS is a for-profit enterprise, all profits are taxed. The estimated tax payments are based on the 1998 business tax schedule.

12. Net Profit/(Loss) Pretax is the gross sales minus total operating expenses.

13. Profit sharing is available only to the manager during the first two years of operation. Since the supervisor will be full-time in year three, he or she will receive profit sharing as well. Profit sharing is based on 2 percent of pretax net profits.

EJS projects a loss of $6,868 during the first year of operation. This projection takes into account potential customers with firms who indicated a strong interest in EJS services. With the highly favorable response to initial marketing and EJS's experience in operating janitorial services, EJS is confident that sales will meet and likely exceed projections.

Note: Although the three-year Profit and Loss Statement shows a sizable net profit, the NFP needs to decide whether the *financial* return on investment and the *mission* return on the investment are sufficient enough to go ahead. This is always a difficult—but essential—decision for social entrepreneurs.

RECAP

In this chapter we covered the all-important issue of how to develop your financials. First, we talked about ways to assure that you get the numbers right. To review, these were as follows:

1. Use an electronic spreadsheet.
2. Consult your financial manager.
3. Include *all* your costs.
4. Have an outside reviewer.

Then, we looked at the sequence you need to use to develop your own financials. These were as follows:

Assemble your financial data.

Analyze your data.

Prepare your financial statements.

I then showed you the financials for Enterprise Janitorial Services, including all of its statements and its assumptions for those statements.

Now you have all the information you need to develop your plan. What's next? Practice time! In the next chapter, I'll give you a chance to apply what you have learned!

QUESTIONS FOR DISCUSSION: CHAPTER 7

1. Do we have the systems internally to give us the data we need to project financials in the manner Peter describes? Do we have ways of finding out all of our costs?

2. Breakeven is so important. Can we do a break-even analysis on our current services?

3. Projecting cash costs of expansion seems like an important thing to do as well. How can we do this for next year's budget to predict the cash cost of areas of growth?

8

Applying the Lessons: A Step-by-Step Business-Planning Exercise

OVERVIEW

In this chapter you will

➤ Apply the business development process to an idea for a new service or expansion.

Now that you have read the process through; learned more about mission, risk, and social entrepreneurism; and now that you have seen how others have applied these techniques to improve their mission capability, it is time for you to do it as well. In this chapter, I'll walk you through the activities that can help you develop a new service or expand your existing ones. I'll give you step-by-step instructions that will allow you to answer the crucial questions that can result in good stewardship decisions for your organization and help you avoid some bad ones.

This chapter is the most hands-on in the book, and I am sure that you will want to use the forms repeatedly. Make copies of the pages and use them.

Note: You may not be ready to go through the intense work that is covered in this chapter. If not, fine. Return to it when you have a venture idea in hand.

A. GETTING READY

This chapter is designed to help you with the most problematic parts of the business-planning process. It assumes that you have already done a lot of work before turning to the forms included here. Before you start using the forms in this chapter, *you should have already done the following:*

Reviewed your mission statement as detailed in Chapter 4, First Steps: Mission Outcomes, Risk, and Idea Generation

Reviewed your willingness to take risks

Decided on a mission outcome and mission-based use of any profits

Selected a group of possible ideas

Generated some business criteria

Selected the best of the ideas using the business

Done some initial investigation into costs, prices, and competition in your preliminary feasibility study

Assuming that you have done those tasks, let's move on. Put the information that you have gathered into Exhibit 8-1, business idea basics, Exhibit 8-2, financial basics, and Exhibit 8-3, pricing basics.

Now let's look at the steps of the process that you should have completed, and what this chapter will provide you. Exhibit 8-4 shows you the outcomes you can expect by completing the materials in this chapter. Note that some parts of the plan will be completed after you finish the chapter, using the information you honed here.

For the remaining sections of this chapter, read each part of the explanatory materials and fill in the forms as best you can. I suggest doing all your work *in pencil,* as you will almost certainly come back and revise things as you move through the forms.

1. Product/Service Definition

What product(s) or service(s) will your new venture or expansion provide? How tightly can you define them? "We will do education" is not a good service definition. Your research in the preliminary feasibility study should have focused you on a more specific definition.

Example: "We will provide legal-aid services to citizens of two new counties."

Example: "We will assist seniors in improving their nutrition by personal counseling in senior centers."

Example: "We will provide testing for birth to three-year-old children for long-term physical disabilities in coordination with our county medical society."

Write a definition of your product(s) or service(s) in the following space:

Exhibit 8-1   Business idea basics.

On this form, fill in the information below as completely as you can.
Product or service description:
Market:
Your expertise in this business:
The mission outcome of the business:
How soon the business should start:
Your profit goal for the business (how much and by when):

Exhibit 8-2   Financial basics.

Item	Cost	Comments

Labor
    Fixed
    Variable		

Administration		
Rent		
Utilities		
Fringe benefits		
Travel		
Equipment		
Licenses		

Marketing
    Advertising
    Printing
    Web site
    Trade show		

Engineering		
Other costs		

Exhibit 8-3   Pricing basics.

Our pricing will be as follows:		
Number	**Unit Price**	**Comments**

Exhibit 8-4 Business plan process review.

Business Development Step	Should Already Be Completed	Will Be Completed in This Chapter	Will Be Completed Later
1. Review your mission statement	—		
2. Assess your willingness to take risk	—		
3. Decide on your mission outcomes from the business	—		
4. Generate your business ideas	—		
5. Develop preliminary feasibility studies	—		
6. Develop a final feasibility study	— Most key questions	— Some final numbers	
7. Develop a business plan		— Most key decisions and financials	— Full written draft
8. Implement the plan			—

_____

_____

_____

_____

2. Definition of the Market

Now that you have defined your product or service, you need to focus on who you will work for, your market. Who are these people? Where are they? How many of them are there? All of these questions should have been discussed already. Again, you want to be as specific as you can.

> *Example:* "Our market for legal aid will be citizens making under $20,000 per year."

> *Example:* "Our market for seniors will be residents of senior housing within 20 miles of our office."

Who will your market be? Write it in the space provided:

_____

_____

_____

_____

3. Definition of the Target Market(s)

Now you need to increase the focus on the market, by targeting a particular segment for your highest research, sales, and customer service efforts. Who will that be for you? Think through a smaller component of the market you listed previously that makes the most business sense for you to target. That target should be the best match between your core competencies and the wants of the market.

> *Example:* "Our target market for legal aid will be people in need of primary legal services. Our secondary market will be seniors in need of legal consumer assistance."

> *Example:* "Our target market for nutrition services will be those seniors referred to us by their physicians. Our secondary market will be other seniors who attend our free educational sessions."

In the following space, list the target market for your business. If you have identified a secondary market focus, list that as well.

_____

_____

_____

_____

4. Listing of Five Core Wants of the Target Market

The next step is to identify the five core wants of your target markets. Once you have done this, you may find that you cannot meet those wants and have to return to a review, and possible revision, of your target markets.

What is it that your markets want? Remember, the issue is *wants* not *needs!* How do you know that these are the markets' wants? Did you ask them, or are you making (perhaps dangerous) assumptions?

Some examples of wants might be flexible hours, lowest possible price, personal treatment, or state-of-the-art services.

List the five core wants of your market on the following lines.

1. _____
2. _____
3. _____
4. _____
5. _____

5. Listing of Core Competencies

You now have your target markets' wants in hand. How will you meet them. Do you have the core competencies that match up with your markets' wants? Let's see.

Market Want: _____ Our Core Competence: _____

Market Want: _____ Our Core Competence: _____

Market Want: _____ Our Core Competence: _____

Market Want: _____ Our Core Competence: _____

Market Want: _____ Our Core Competence: _____

Do your competencies match up well to meet the wants of the target markets? If not, you may want to go back to step 3 and change your target market, or you may need to find ways to strengthen or acquire certain competencies, which may increase your costs.

6. Reaching the Markets

How will you establish relations with your market(s)? This includes not just sales, but doing regular customer research, developing long-term relationships, and, of course, promotion and sales. What tactics will you use? If you are entering a new market, how will you establish a beachhead?

Examples could be trade show presentations, cold calls, referrals, advertising, or some other outreach function.

List how you plan to reach out to, and stay in touch with, your markets:

_____

_____

_____

_____

7. The Mission Outcomes of the Business

This is a crucial step. Now that you have defined your business, what will the mission outcome of the business be? Some specific mission service? Profit to do more direct mission? A combination?

List your expectations in the following space in as specific a manner as possible.

_____

_____

_____

_____

B. KEY FINANCIALS

In this section, we'll cover the development of the key financials. Let's start with a quick review of the terminology we'll be using.

1. Start-up Costs

How much are you putting at risk? What costs are there that will be incurred before your business opens, and after it opens, during the remaining start-up period? Where will this money come from?

Your first job is to complete Exhibit 8-5, the start-up cost form. Be vigilant about including every possible start-up cost: training, rent, licensing, legal, accounting, loan fees, equipment, raw materials, packaging, production design and engineering, and so forth.

2. Initial Size of the Business

What is your initial size going to be in terms of units of production, revenue, employees, and space? All businesses have a size below which it doesn't make sense to operate. On the other hand, you can have starting goals that are too high for you to afford in working capital, sales staff, production capacity, or administrative support. You should complete Exhibit 8-6, the form on initial size, and then review the implications of that size in terms of market demand, production capacity, personnel, and

Exhibit 8-5   Start-up cost estimation.

Start-up Cost Estimation	
Cost Item	Cost Estimate
Wages	
Benefits	
Training	
Rent	
Utilities	
Equipment (detail)	
Supplies	
Licenses	
Marketing (detail)	
Printing	
Travel	
Raw materials	
Engineering	
Legal	
Accounting	
Total Start-up Costs	

finance. If any of these four areas conflict with your initial assessment, now is an excellent time to revise your starting size.

3. Fixed Costs

Once you know the starting size, you can fill in your fixed costs form. Remember, *fixed costs* are the costs that don't change when sales go up (or down). Rent, utilities, depreciation, insurance, and administrative overhead are examples of fixed costs. Take those numbers and apply them to the initial size of your business by filling out Exhibit 8-7.

4. Variable Costs

Variable costs refer to costs that change with sales volume. Direct labor, raw materials, waste, shipping, and consumable supplies are all examples of

Exhibit 8-6   Initial size of business.

Initial Size of Our Business			
	Year One	**Year Two**	**Year Three**
Sales (in units of sale)			
Sales (in dollars)			

Rationale: *The reason we think we need to be this size to start* is as follows:

Checklist: *Will our market support this size? Can we produce this much product or service? Can we do it with a high level of quality and customer satisfaction?*

NOTES:

variable costs. Your job is to list all of your variable costs for each unit of sale on Exhibit 8-8. The key here is to be as precise and detailed as possible.

5. Volume Projections

On the volume projection form (Exhibit 8-9), list the number of units of service you expect to provide per month for the first year and per quarter for the next two. Remember that being overly optimistic *or* pessimistic here will hurt your ability to price accurately and, more importantly, competitively. If you are planning to sell more than one service, use the multiple forms provided. This form has the most benefit if you are charging per unit of service.

6. Cash Flow Projections

This form (Exhibit 8-10) will take a bit of time and attention. You can do it by hand, on the following form, or adapt it to a spreadsheet on your computer.

Exhibit 8-7   Fixed costs estimation.

Fixed Cost Item	Cost Estimation per Year		
	YR 1	YR 2	YR 3
Wages			
Fringes			
Rent			
Utilities			
Depreciation			
Marketing			
Legal			
Printing			
Travel			
Administration			
Total Fixed Costs per Year			

NOTES:

Exhibit 8-8   Variable cost estimation.

Variable Cost Item	Cost Estimate per Item
Direct labor	
Direct fringes	
Raw materials	
Supplies	
Direct travel	
Direct utilities	
Direct shipping	
Waste	
Direct phone	
Total Variable Cost per Item	

Exhibit 8-9 Volume projection.

First Item Volume Projection:

Month	1	2	3	4	5	6	7	8	9	10	11	12
Sales Units Yr 1												
Quarter	First			Second			Third			Fourth		
Year 2												
Year 3												

Second Item Volume Projection:

Month	1	2	3	4	5	6	7	8	9	10	11	12
Sales Units Yr 1												
Quarter	First			Second			Third			Fourth		
Year 2												
Year 3												

Third Item Volume Projection:

Month	1	2	3	4	5	6	7	8	9	10	11	12
Sales Units Yr 1												
Quarter	First			Second			Third			Fourth		
Year 2												
Year 3												

Fourth Item Volume Projection:

Month	1	2	3	4	5	6	7	8	9	10	11	12
Sales Units Yr 1												
Quarter	First			Second			Third			Fourth		
Year 2												
Year 3												

Remember, cash is different from income and expense. On this form, you want to include all of your receipts and all of your disbursements in the month (or quarter) in which they actually are received or disbursed. Depreciation is not a cash expense. Debt service (including interest and principal) is. Loans that you receive should be included in your receipts.

You will note that the form includes your start-up costs and initial start-up capital. You should be able to retrieve the costs from your start-up cost form that you filled out earlier.

Exhibit 8-10 Your business pro forma cash flow analysis for year one.

MONTH	1	2	3	4	5	6	7	8	9	10	11	12	TTL
UNITS OF SALE PER MONTH													
CASH RECEIPTS													
DISBURSEMENTS													
Variable labor													
Variable payroll/fringe													
Supplies													
Advertising													
Vehicle operation													
Repairs													
Insurance													
Legal and accounting													
Salaries													
Loan													
Telephone													
Rent/utilities													
TOTAL DISBURSEMENTS													
NET CASH FLOW													
CUMULATIVE CASH FLOW													
STARTING CASH ON HAND													
CASH RECEIPTS													
CASH DISBURSEMENTS													
ENDING CASH ON HAND													

Exhibit 8-11   Pricing chart.

Item	Cost	Instructions
Fixed Costs per Year		
Units of Sales per Year		
Fixed Cost per Unit		Divide the Fixed Costs per Year by the Units of Sales per Year to arrive at Fixed Cost per Unit
Variable Cost per Unit		
Profit per Unit		
Total Price per Unit		Add up the per unit costs to get the total price per unit

Enter the information, then do the addition and subtraction. If you are doing this by hand, *do it in pencil!* It is almost certain that you will revise this form.

Are there months in which you run out of cash? Are there months in which your cash is critically low? If so, you may need to go back and revise the amount of cash you need to start with. Don't forget to take into account the amount of time your customer will take to pay you after you deliver the product or service. A sale in April, for example, may not result in cash in your checking account until June.

7. Pricing—Single Item

If your business is going to start with just one product or service, this section is for you. If you have more than one, go directly to the next subsection.

As you build your price, remember, it is composed of four parts: fixed costs, variable costs, profit, and market forces. The first three raise the price, the fourth holds it down or even reduces it. Also remember that the amount of fixed costs that you allocate to each unit of sale is dependent on how many sales you expect each year. If your sales projections turn out to have been unreasonably optimistic, you will not have recovered all your fixed costs. If they wind up having been too low, you may well have had to price higher than you should have in a highly competitive marketplace. So be careful.

But, do your best to add *all* of your costs into the price, and be sure to add a profit! If the price you decide upon is different than what you started with earlier in this chapter, you may need to revise your cash flows! (See Exhibit 8-11.)

8. Pricing—Multiple Services

The issues in pricing many services, or an array of services, are similar to a single item, but they have one crucial issue that is different: the spread of your fixed costs. Look at the following example, and then fill in the form for your own array of products or services. The form provided in Exhibit 8-12 is designed for a maximum of four products or services. If you have more, just hand draw a similar form with more columns.

Remember, the core components of price remain the same: fixed costs, variable costs, profit, and the market. I've included an example (Exhibit 8-13) to help you with this important form.

9. Breakeven

Now you are ready for a heads-up check on your work to this point: a break-even analysis. We have included a form for you to do this for one

Exhibit 8-12   Multiple-service pricing.

Total Fixed Costs per Year for the Business : _____

	Service 1	Service 2	Service 3	Service 4
Fixed Cost % Allocation				
Fixed Costs				
Units of Sale				
Fixed Cost per Unit				
Variable Cost per Unit				
Profit per Unit				
Price per Unit				

Exhibit 8-13 Example of multiple-service pricing.

Total Fixed Costs per Year for the Business : $100,000

	Item 1	Item 2	Item 3	Item 4
Fixed Cost % Allocation	20	15	40	25
Fixed Costs	$20,000	$15,000	$40,000	$25,000
Units of Sale	10,000	16,500	27,500	12,000
Fixed Cost per Unit	$2.00	$0.91	$1.45	$2.08
Variable Cost per Unit	$0.21	$0.11	$0.45	$0.17
Profit per Unit	$0.05	$0.10	$0.17	$0.22
Price per Unit	$2.26	$1.12	$2.07	$2.47

product or for multiple products. Break-even analysis is designed to show you how many units of sale you need to recover all your costs at a certain mix of costs and price. If you find that your cost/price mix takes too long to recover, you may need to move your price up (if the market will bear that) or move your costs down (if you can). Understanding breakeven is important to ongoing business operations as well. It will allow you to quickly assess the impact of discounting or price cutting to retain business.

Variable cost per unit: _____

Price per unit: _____

Fixed cost per year: _____

$$\text{Breakeven} = \frac{\text{Fixed Cost}}{(\text{Price} - \text{Variable Cost})}$$

Calculate the breakeven now for your product. Can you provide that much service, or manufacture that much product? How soon? Will the market bear this amount of sales?

10. Income and Expense Projections

Now we need to start our income and expense sheets. Don't despair—much of the information is already gathered.

Use the following form to enter your data for your first year of business by month (Exhibit 8-14), and then for the next two years by quarter. Complete the first year, and then work your way by quarters in the latter forms.

Remember that this should be an accrual form. Put the income in when the sales transaction occurs, and the same for expenses. Interest only, no repayment of debt principal. Depreciation instead of capital purchases.

11. Working Capital Needs

Working capital is the money you need to operate your business between the time you provide a service or deliver a product and you receive payment. The larger your business and/or the longer your customers take to pay you, the more working capital you require. As your business grows, you will need more cash in working capital. Where will it come from? Exhibit 8-15 and your cash flow projections will tell you.

Note that in years two and three, you compute working capital needed by replacing total sales with the difference (growth) in sales from years one and two. All other calculations remain the same.

C. BUSINESS-PLANNING SEQUENCE

Now, at last, you are ready to plan. In the sheets provided in Exhibit 8-16 list the sequence of events that must occur for your business to become a

Exhibit 8-14   Income and expense projections.

Month	1	2	3	4	5	6	7	8	9	10	11	12	Total
GROSS SALES													
OPERATING EXPENSES													
Salaries													
Variable labor													
Fringe benefits and payroll taxes													
Materials and supplies													
Telephone													
Legal/accounting													
Advertising													
Rent/utilities													
Depreciation													
Insurance													
Licenses													
Repairs													
Vehicle operation and maintenance													
Interest													
TOTAL OPERATING EXPENSES													
PROFIT(LOSS)													
EARNINGS TO DATE													

Exhibit 8-15   Working capital.

	Working Capital Needs — Year One		
Item	**Item Need**		**Total Needs**
Projected Income			
Days to Payment			
Total Working Capital Needed (Income × (Days to Payment/365))	**(Copy Sum →)**		
Additional Cash Needs—Year One			
Equipment Purchases			
Minus Loans	(	)	
Start-up Costs			
Total Additional Cash Needs	**(Copy Sum →)**		
Total Cash Needed—Year One			

reality. Add some tentative dates and who you will assign to complete the task. Do this list in pencil, as it is almost certain to change. Think through all the things that have to happen, and list them here.

Example Task List

	Task to Be Completed	Deadline	Person Assigned
1	Talk to banker about loan	8/1	Mike
2	Estimate debt from cash flow	7/15	Eric
3	Talk to board members about risk	7/1	Sally

With this list, which was written down as people thought about things, the writer would first need to revise and put things in order. Then from this list, develop goals for your business. The idea of the sequence list is to get all the activities down in front of you, and this will enable you to gather the work into goals and objectives.

Remember: *A goal* is a statement of desired outcome. It may or may not be quantified or have a deadline. An *objective* has to include four things:

1. Support of the goal
2. A quantified outcome
3. A deadline
4. A person responsible for its achievement

The preceding example of activities might turn into the goal and objectives which follow:

Goal One: Obtain Adequate Financing for Business

Objective	Deadline	Costs (hrs)	Person Responsible
1. Estimate total debt needs for project	7/1	Staff time (10)	Eric
2. Meet with board to discuss acceptable risk	7/15	Staff and board time (1)	Sally and Eric
3. Meet with banker	7/20	Staff time (2)	Eric and Mike
4. Develop loan application	7/30	Staff time (8)	Eric and Mike
5. Present loan application	8/15	Staff time (1)	Eric and Mike

Exhibit 8-16   Task list.

	Task to Be Completed	Deadline	Person Assigned
1			
2			
3			
4			
5			
6			
7			
8			
9			
10			
11			
12			
13			
14			
15			
16			
17			
18			
19			
20			
21			
22			
23			
24			

Exhibit 8-16   Continued

Goal One:			
Objective	Deadline	Costs	Person Responsible
1.			
2.			
3.			
4.			
5.			

<u>Notes on Goal One:</u>

Goal Two:			
Objective	Deadline	Costs	Person Responsible
1.			
2.			
3.			
4.			
5.			

<u>Notes on Goal Two:</u>

Exhibit 8-16   Continued

Goal Three:			
Objective	**Deadline**	**Costs**	**Person Responsible**
1.			
2.			
3.			
4.			
5.			

Notes on Goal Three:

Goal Four:			
Objective	**Deadline**	**Costs**	**Person Responsible**
1.			
2.			
3.			
4.			
5.			

Notes on Goal Four:

Exhibit 8-16   Continued

Goal Five:

Objective	Deadline	Costs	Person Responsible
1.			
2.			
3.			
4.			
5.			

<u>Notes on Goal Five:</u>

Goal Six:

Objective	Deadline	Costs	Person Responsible
1.			
2.			
3.			
4.			
5.			

<u>Notes on Goal Six:</u>

Exhibit 8-16   Continued

Goal Seven:			
Objective	**Deadline**	**Costs**	**Person Responsible**
1.			
2.			
3.			
4.			
5.			

<u>Notes on Goal Seven:</u>

Goal Eight:			
Objective	**Deadline**	**Costs**	**Person Responsible**
1.			
2.			
3.			
4.			
5.			

<u>Notes on Goal Eight:</u>

Exhibit 8-16   Continued

Goal Nine:			
Objective	**Deadline**	**Costs**	**Person Responsible**
1.			
2.			
3.			
4.			
5.			

<u>Notes on Goal Nine:</u>

Goal Ten:			
Objective	**Deadline**	**Costs**	**Person Responsible**
1.			
2.			
3.			
4.			
5.			

<u>Notes on Goal Ten:</u>

Add as many of the following as you can: objectives, costs, assigned personnel.

Congratulations! You have completed the bulk of the work needed to write your business plan. Now you need to take that information and put it into a business plan outline like the one used in Chapter 6, The Business Plan.

RECAP

In this chapter, we have put our learning to use by actually answering many of the questions and solving many of the problems you will have to deal with in deciding about your new business or expansion. While there is a lot of work still to be done after this information is gathered, the toughest issues have almost certainly been dealt with.

QUESTIONS FOR DISCUSSION: CHAPTER 8

1. Should we run through these forms now in a mock planning exercise, or wait until we actually have a business idea or expansion to consider?

2. After looking at the information that is needed, what additional training, information systems, or other resources do we need?

9

Financing Your Entrepreneurship

OVERVIEW

In this chapter you will learn about the following:

- ➤ Assessing Your Financing Needs
- ➤ Methods of Financing
- ➤ Sources of Financing
- ➤ Rules for Financing
- ➤ Dealing with Lenders

Your new or expanded service will always need financing. Social entrepreneurs know that expanding or developing new services always costs money. But, where will that money come from, and what form will it take? That's the subject of this chapter.

First, we'll look at how you can assess your financing needs. You will learn how to look at growth, working capital, start-up costs, and capital investments and estimate how much you will need.

Second, we'll turn to the issue of the choices you have in financing. You can borrow short term or long term, and from a variety of sources. The important thing is to match the financing need with the appropriate financing type.

Third, we'll go through all the myriad of financing sources that you can tap. There seem to be more of these every day, and I'll give you a listing that you can use to start with.

Fourth, we will look at some rules for financing. They may not be the rules you expect, but they can really save your organization a lot of money.

And last, we'll look at the challenges in working with lenders, how to invest some time and effort now to ease the loan acquisition process later.

By the end of the chapter, you will not be a graduate finance major from an elite business school, but you will know what you need to know about financing to help you on your entrepreneurial quest.

But before we get into the specifics, a little ranting on my part is necessary. My primary rule of borrowing is this:

Never, ever borrow if you are losing money. Only borrow if you are making money or if your business plan projects a profit.

Does that sound strange? Why, if you are making money would you need to borrow? For a lot of reasons, including start-up costs, financing rapid growth, and mission-based leveraging of assets, all of which we'll cover in the first section of this chapter. But the key here is to understand this: *All loans are paid back from profits, not from losses.* This is an absolute, irrevocable rule of your balance sheet. If your organization has ever had a debt, and if that debt is now paid off, or at least paid down a bit, your organization made a profit between then and now. Borrowing to cover temporary cash shortfalls is fine, and we'll cover ways to do that. But borrowing to cover losses is not, to say the least, good stewardship. It is the first step on a short path to bankruptcy.

Is borrowing risky? Inherently, yes. You may not have adequate cash in the future to pay back the loan. As social entrepreneurs learn to assess the risks for their ventures well, they also learn the techniques of financing those ventures, and how to match up the venture with the financing technique. But the bottom line is that, to keep your creditors happy, you must make money. Never forget that.

A. ASSESSING YOUR FINANCING NEEDS

No one wants to borrow money unless they need to. This is true for us as individuals, and certainly it is good stewardship to keep our borrowing to a minimum. But, in some cases, a social entrepreneur knows that it is better to borrow for a project than to use up all available cash, as long as that project will show net revenue or profit, as was noted previously. But how do you figure out how much you need, or when to borrow it? There are three tools that will help you, and you have already been exposed to them in Chapters 7 and 8, Business Plan Financial Projections and Applying the Lessons: A Step-by-Step Business-Planning Exercise, when you learned how to develop your financials. Let's go through the sequence of looking at your needs in order.

1. What Are Your Start-up Costs?

The first task is to look at the costs you will incur before you begin the business. They will, by definition, not be offset by income, because you

Exhibit 9-1   Start-up cost estimation.

Start-up Cost Estimation	
Cost Item	Cost Estimate
Wages	$14,250.00
Benefits	1,225.50
Training	2,410.00
Rent	3,560.00
Utilities	0
Equipment (detail)	190,500.00
Supplies	3,100.00
Licenses	0
Marketing (detail)	2,954.00
Printing	1,240.00
Travel	0
Raw materials	0
Engineering	0
Legal	2,000.00
Accounting	1,675.00
Total Start-up Costs	**$222,914.50**

haven't started your new service yet! The chart you used in the last chapter looked like the one in Exhibit 9-1. I've filled in the information here to give us a sample to discuss.

You see that the out-of-pocket start-up costs for this business are nearly $223,000. And, as you will see later in the chapter, there are different kinds of debt for different kinds of needs. As it stands, these people need an equipment loan, and then a source of funds to cover start-up costs. But, that's just the first step. Now we need to look at their working capital needs.

2. Working Capital Estimation
Working capital is the amount of money you need to operate your service between the time you provide a service or deliver a product and you get paid. The amount of working capital your new or expanded business needs depends on two things: how much volume of service (and, thus, of money) you are doing, and how long your customers take to pay you. The faster

you grow, the more working capital you need. The longer your customers hang on to your bills before paying, the more working capital you need. If a service you have grows a lot in one year, it eats up cash, and that is working capital. Remember the scenario I showed you in Chapter 2, The Benefits of the Social Entrepreneurism Model, the one about the $1 million no-risk contract? Remember that it ate up over $200,000 in cash before the agency got paid, and their payment time was only 75 days? But if the contract had been $2 million, the cash need would have doubled. Or, if the payor had decided to pay in 90 days, the working capital needed would have gone up by a third. So what do you do to figure this out? Run the numbers. The chart in Exhibit 9-2 was one we used in Chapter 8, Applying the Lessons: A Step-by-Step Business-Planning Exercise. Again, I've filled it in for this hypothetical business to make a few points.

You can see that this chart also allows you to enter the amount of your loan or loans, and then have a net figure that you need to cover from your organization or from other sources. And, while this provides excellent information, it is not the end of the estimation. The cash needs of our hypothetical organization could actually be worse than this, a lot worse. Why? Because the number in Exhibit 9-2 is estimated on an *annual* basis—for the first year of the business. The reality of the business is on a day-to-day, or month-to-month basis. Early on, this can mean some real cash holes. For example, sales in the first few months will probably lag way behind sales later in the year. Thus, the $220,000 projected income

Exhibit 9-2   Working capital.

Working Capital Needs—Year One		
Item	Item Need	Total Needs
Projected Annual Income	$220,000.00	
Days to Payment	45	
Total Working Capital Needed *(Income × (Days to Payment/365))*	(Copy Sum →)	$27,123.29
Additional Cash Needs—Year One		
Equipment Purchases	$190,500.00	
Minus Loans	(enter)	
Start-up Costs	$32,414.50	
Total Additional Cash Needs	(Copy Sum →)	$222,914.50
Total Cash Needed-Year One		$250,037.79

will almost certainly not be divided neatly into 12 equal monthly parts, and this will probably lead to more cash problems. How do we check this? By using our cash flow projection.

3. Checking with the Cash Flow Projection

Our third stop on the financial needs projection journey is to look carefully at the monthly cash flow projection that was developed during the business development process. It should tell us a great deal about the actual cash shortfalls we may encounter. In Exhibit 9-3, I've put together an abbreviated cash flow projection for our hypothetical business. I've condensed the number of lines, too, and only projected out six months. I've given the organization a starting cash number that is negative and represents the total of the start-up costs and equipment purchases shown in Exhibit 9-1. For the purposes of this example, a unit of service will eventually result in $10 for the organization. That means they are projecting 22,000 units of service provided by the end of the year. That would be 1,833 units per month if it were steady throughout the year, but start-ups are never steady. Disbursements are shown as fairly steady, since nearly all of the expenses are salaries and fringes, and go out regularly, no matter what money has been received. The service also projects a $19,000 profit at the end of the first year, which is excellent, but should be a cautionary tale to you as you read this: Even profitable organizations need cash. How much worse would this be if they were only trying to break even?

Check it out. According to our annual estimate in Exhibit 9-2, this organization should only have a problem that is $250,000 in size. According to the cash flow, it is even bigger, over $280,000 in the red.

☞ **HANDS ON:** And it may be worse than this. Dozens of social entrepreneurs that I have worked with have made the same, understandable mistake: assuming that the number of days it takes to get paid is too low. This doesn't have to happen because the customer is lying; you may not be asking the right information. Do this. When you talk to customers about how long it will take to get paid, ask for an average number of days that they hold your bill before processing it. Let's say their answer is this, "Our policy is to pay all bills in 30 days." So, you go and put the number 30 into Exhibit 9-2. And you are in real trouble. Because what the customers don't tell you is that they pay 30 days after the bills are posted, and that only happens at the end of the month, or on the 15th, or on some other date. So, if you bill at the end of June, and they get the bill in early July and then don't post until July 30, they don't cut you a check until August 28, and you don't get the check until September 5th or so, which is 67 days from June 30. This, to say the

Exhibit 9-3 Cash flow projection.

	Month 1	Month 2	Month 3	Month 4	Month 5	Month 6
Units of Services	*400*	*600*	*900*	*1,200*	*1,800*	*2,350*
Receipts	$0	$2,000	$5,000	$8,500	$10,500	$15,000
Disbursements	($16,750)	($16,750)	($16,750)	($16,750)	($16,750)	($16,750)
Cash Flow	($16,750)	($14,750)	($11,750)	($8,250)	($6,250)	($1,250)
Starting Cash	($222,915)	($239,665)	($254,415)	($266,165)	($274,415)	($280,665)
Ending Cash	($239,665)	($254,415)	($266,165)	($274,415)	($280,665)	($281,915)

least, is a cash problem. So ask for the number of days to payment, and then add, "From when? When you get the bill, post the bill, or some other time?" Your estimates will be much, much more accurate.

Using these three steps you can zero in on how much cash you will really need. For this organization, we still need $190,000 or so in equipment, and about $90,000 in start-up and working capital funds, and that is only if our projections are *really* accurate.

☞ **HANDS ON:** Projections are just educated guesses. Remember to leave some cushion in your cash projections. This will mean that you need to borrow more, or start with more money on hand, but it will give you some ability to sleep at night. I wish I could give you a formula. Many organizations try to never dip into their cash below a 30-day cushion. Some go as low as 15 days. Obviously, the more cushion you have, the more expensive it is, and, at some point, you won't be able to borrow a high amount of cushion at all. Just remember to keep some cash on hand. The financial people's term for this is *contingency,* which is their way of acknowledging Murphy's Law. And Murphy does live.

Thus, the amount the agency may want to have on hand at the start of the project may be in excess of $300,000 or so with a contingency fund. Where will it come from? How will we match up financing needs with appropriate sources? What are the sources and the different methods of financing a new or expanding business? The next two sections will tell you the answers to these very important questions.

B. METHODS OF FINANCING

Choices, choices, choices. In the financial bazaars of today you have so many different choices that it can be overwhelming at times. This section will help you wind your way through the maze of financing choices and will also help you get ready before you visit a potential lender.

1. Before You See the Lender

Even though you can borrow in a wide variety of ways, there are still five primary things lenders will want to know when you approach them for a loan. These five things are as follows:

- The purpose of the loan
- The collateral
- How much your organization will contribute

- What you will do to pay back the loan
- How long you will take to pay it back

Let's look at each in detail.

a. What is the purpose of the loan? As you will see in a few pages, there are different kinds of loans for different kinds of needs. To help us walk through this section, let's use the hypothetical agency venture I showed you in the section on estimating your financing needs, the organization that needed $190,000 for equipment. We don't know the kind of equipment (vehicles, computers, manufacturing equipment, or some other type) or how fast it will be depreciated, but for purposes of this example, let's focus on the equipment loan. All lenders will first ask about the purpose of your loan, so make sure you have broken out the needs into appropriate categories. Our hypothetical agency would also need nearly $90,000 in working capital at a minimum, more if it adds in a contingency. These are fundamentally different purposes, they are paid back differently, and have different collateralization. Try not to group different financing needs together.

b. Is collateral available? *Collateral* is what your organization puts up to secure the loan. In the case of a default on the loan, the lender takes the collateral and tries to turn it into cash to recapture some or even all of its loan. For example, when you take out a mortgage on a house or a loan on a new car, while you hold the title, there is something called a *lien* on that title that says that you cannot sell the house or the car until the lien is paid off. What that really means is that if you don't pay the loan, the lender gets your car or house. The car or house is the collateral. For equipment and buildings, the kind of collateral is pretty straightforward—it will be the building or the equipment. For a working capital loan, it may well be *all* your receivables, or even *all* your organizational assets. The lender will try to push for as much collateral as possible, as this reduces its risk.

☞ **HANDS ON:** This is really important. In the lending process, *everything is negotiable.* A little later in the chapter we'll discuss working with lenders, but always remember that a loan is a business deal, and all business deals have room to negotiate. While it is reasonable for a lender to ask for collateral, some lenders will ask for a ridiculous amount of this kind of security. Do not automatically agree. Consider the impact carefully before you take the loan. I am not suggesting that you should gripe about everything in a loan package, just that you should remember that nothing is set in stone *until you sign the agreement.* Then you have to live with what you agreed to. Think before you sign.

❏ **FOR EXAMPLE:** Here are some of the things that I have negotiated in helping not-for-profits borrow: the length of the loan, the interest rate, a delay in debt service repayment, a reduction in cosigners (particularly board members), a reduction in down payment, a removal of 80 percent of collateral, the term of the loan, and the position of the lender in relation to other creditors. Again, *everything is negotiable* until you sign the paperwork. That does not mean that the lender will agree, but a good steward will try to get the best deal possible, and it is a *very* competitive marketplace out there.

Remember, this is not a relationship where lenders are royalty while you are some sort of vassal seeking their favor. The bank is *selling you money.* You are the *customer* and thus higher, not lower, on the food chain. Act like it.

c. How much will you contribute? Here is another risk reducer for the lender. On nearly all loans, your organization will have to show that you are sharing the risk through a down payment. The more you pay up front, the happier the lender will almost always be. Of course, the more you pay up front, the more cash you use up (and can't use for other purposes), so again put this item into your negotiation list. If cash flow is going to be particularly strong and you can demonstrate that, perhaps a lower down payment would be possible. If interest rates are pretty high, perhaps a higher down payment makes more sense. Each loan will be unique. So think, strategize, and negotiate. But expect to pay something up front.

☞ **HANDS ON:** Down-payment-free loans have a dark side as well. They can lure you in with the attractiveness of a cash-free loan. Kind of like a credit card in the mail that tells you that you have been preapproved for a $5,000 limit. A no-down-payment loan means that your monthly payments will be higher, and your monthly interest costs will be much higher to start. Can your cash flow support the higher debt service? Make sure before you agree to what appears to be a great deal. If it seems too good to be true, it almost always is.

d. How will you pay back the loan? I know, I know, the answer you are thinking is, Won't we pay it back in dollars? But the question goes to a more subtle issue: Will the loan's purpose generate adequate cash flow to pay off the loan? In other words, will you pay back the loan from profits generated from the new or expanded service?

❏ **FOR EXAMPLE:** Let's look at a socially entrepreneurial organization that wants to expand its transportation services for the elderly. The state Department on Aging agrees to pay the agency a monthly fee to transport seniors, but the agency has to finance the purchase and operation of the vans. Each of the accessible vans cost $50,000 to purchase, $5,000 a year to insure, and $22,000 to operate, including staff time and administrative costs, for a total of $27,000 annually. The agency goes to the bank and asks for a $45,000 loan (having agreed to pay 10 percent in cash). The loan is a four-year note at 6 percent, which results in a monthly payment of $1,369, or $16,428 per year. Thus, the agency would have to get at least *$17,000 more than the annual operating costs of $27,000* to be able to show the bank that the van can generate the cash to pay back the loan.

This underscores the first rule I told you about at the beginning of the chapter—*don't borrow unless you are making money.* In this case, the van is what needs to make money to justify the loan to both the borrower and the lender. Otherwise, the loan will likely wind up in default. And it also emphasizes the need to work with funders who will allow you to make a profit so that you can finance your expanded services.

e. How long will it take for you to pay it back? Most loans for equipment or buildings have a natural length—and it is less than the time it takes the equipment or building to wear out and lose all of its value. The reason for this is pretty simple if you look at it from the lender's point of view. The further out in time you go, the less and less sure the lender is that you can pay back a loan—who *really* knows what the future will bring? The lender knows that you are much less likely to default early in the loan term than later and wants to make sure that the loan is all recovered well before the collateral wears out, so that if the lender has to sell the collateral, it will at least get *some* cash for it.

Working capital loans are much tougher to put a time on, and much will depend on the quality of your business plan, and how far out you project your financials. If you only go out two years instead of three, don't anticipate a bank jumping in for a three-year loan. In fact, for some financing, you may have to develop financials much longer than the three years I suggested to you in Chapter 7, Business Plan Financial Projections.

Remember this: Longer is more expensive in terms of interest. A lot more expensive. A longer loan lowers your monthly debt service, but nails you in terms of total cost. Lenders are really torn on this one: Shorter loans are less risky than longer ones for a particular customer, but longer ones generate more interest (and thus income) particularly in the first years of the loan. Lenders want their profits, but they also want to keep their risk reasonable. You are on the same teeter-totter: You want low payments but also low total loan costs. Later in this chapter, we'll talk about my rules for borrowing, and I come down on the side that shorter is *almost always* better.

These five items are the main things you need to consider *before you go see a lender.* They will be the crux of your discussions and your negotiations. Think them through early, and don't be surprised when you get asked about them.

2. Kinds of Debt
There are five core kinds of debt that are available from traditional lenders, with dozens of variations within each main type. We'll review the basic tenets of each type now, and then turn to some less traditional, but no less useful, sources of financing.

a. Lines of credit. Lines of credit are loans that are preapproved before you need them, based on an expectation of a seasonal cash need. For example, retailers need cash to buy inventory every summer for delivery in the early fall so that they can sell their stock during the Christmas season. The inventory must be paid for at purchase or at delivery, but the cash won't show up from the customer until November or December. These retailers borrow in the summer and early fall, and pay back the loan as the cash comes in.

For your organization, a seasonal cash need might be at the time of year when your largest funder (perhaps a government) hasn't gotten around to cutting your contract, and you go a month without your biggest income check. Having a line of credit is prudent, but you are not allowed to use it like a long-term loan. The lender will expect you to *rest* the line (pay the balance down to zero) annually for at least 30 days to show that you are not using it as long-term financing.

☞ **HANDS ON:** Here's what you do to get your line of credit. Look at your cash flow experience for the past year, and then at your cash flow projection for the coming six months. Talk with your treasurer and your accountant about what a prudent amount of credit would be. Then go see your banker, and show him or her your estimates. If the banker agrees that having a line of credit makes sense for you, he or she will set up a line of credit for you. Let's say your line is set up for $40,000. On some future payday when your largest check has not arrived and you normally would be sweating making payroll, you just call the banker, and ask for the amount you need to be transferred into your checking account. The bank does it instantly. On Monday, the check arrives, and you deposit it, paying off the amount you borrowed on Friday, plus a very small amount in interest. Thus, lines make borrowing a whole lot easier and significantly less expensive. If you had to take out a 30-day note to cover payroll, you would be paying more and be a whole lot more stressed.

☞ **HANDS ON:** Remember that lines of credit, like so many other kinds of financing, are very competitive. You can expect to pay interest of prime rate plus a point or point and a half, but never agree to pay an annual fee to hold a line open. If a lender tries that, go somewhere else.

☞ **HANDS ON:** Lines of credit are a kind of access to cash that I think all social entrepreneurs should have. But, please remember that lines are like credit cards: You can get into trouble quickly by using the line to cover up deeper, more systemic problems. It's very tempting to just borrow a bit on the line instead of taking harder actions such as laying off staff, cutting back hours, or even discontinuing a service that is becoming a black hole of losses. Here's how to put a very healthy check and balance into place. Establish a policy that the executive director must check in by phone or fax with the board treasurer or president before drawing down any funds on the line. I don't mean for this double-checking to slow the process down; it should just be a quick call that notifies the board member why the draw is being made, and for how much. Remember, the board members are fiduciaries, and ultimately responsible for all loans. Most boards require board approval before any other kind of borrowing, but they leave the line of credit decisions to the staff. Don't follow their lead. Keep the check and balance system healthy. It protects both board and staff.

b. Equipment financing. This type of loan is designed for purchasing equipment and is made with the equipment in question as collateral. The loan term is set, as I said earlier for slightly less that the useful life of the equipment, which can range from three to 15 years depending on the type of equipment used for collateral and how easily it can be turned into cash. Remember that you will need to prove to the lender that the equipment can bring in enough money to pay for its operation and maintenance and *still* pay off the loan. And, you'll need to pay a significant down payment, usually 15 to 20 percent.

☞ **HANDS ON:** One thing that most lenders hate to lend for is computer equipment. Why? Because it loses its value so incredibly fast. If your organization were to buy five computers today and default in six months on a loan taken out to buy them, how much money would the bank get if it repossessed the computers and tried to sell them? Not much. So, don't expect a lot of smiles if you go to a lender for a loan that is just for computers, printers, servers, or other high-tech equipment.

c. Working capital financing. This type of loan helps a new business (or newly expanded service) meet its cash needs until retained earnings accumulate. We've spent a fair amount of time discussing your working capital needs, and how big they can quickly be. Working capital loans absolutely cannot be obtained without a business plan, and the bank will want a lot of collateral in the form of your receivables and perhaps some other assets. The interest rate for this type of debt is prime plus 2 percent or more. Working capital loans are often difficult to obtain from traditional lenders because of the risk level involved, so I suggest that you seek them from economic development lenders, and only try to get them if you can demonstrate the development of a number of new jobs through your new business or expansion.

d. Economic development financing. This type of loan comes from a variety of sources including the Small Business Administration, your state commerce department, and city or county development agencies. Interest is usually charged at much lower than market rates. This type of loan is mixed with standard commercial lending and may be a good vehicle for capital if you are creating new jobs, hiring minority employees, or locating your business venture in an enterprise zone. Each locale has different criteria for this type of loan or loan guarantee, so be sure to check with your banker and your mayor's office for information on what is available to you in your location.

☞ **HANDS ON:** Economic development can be summarized in three words: *jobs, jobs,* and *jobs.* If you are creating jobs, the people at economic development *want* to talk to you. Don't walk in and say, "I'm a poor not-for-profit and I'm looking for cheap money." Walk in and tell them, "I'm creating 10 (20, 30, 40) jobs. I have to decide where to locate this new business. What can you do for me?"

❑ **FOR EXAMPLE:** About 10 years ago, I was helping a client organization that was starting a print shop (to do duplicating and custom printing) that would employ welfare recipients as a method of training them to get them off of public payments. Once the business plan was complete, we called the mayor's office and set up a meeting. When we met with the mayor and her chief of staff, we told them about the business and that we would be creating, over the next two years, nearly 25 new full-time jobs. We asked them what they could do to help. Usually in these situations, you find out about a low-interest loan, or a tax abatement for a landlord, or even a grant of some kind. Not this time. In an hour we walked out with:

- Rent-free space in a vacant city-owned building for two years
- A no-interest working capital loan that was spread over five years
- A 2 percent loan for two-thirds of our equipment needs
- $155,000 in city printing contracts—which was over 20 percent of our first year income projections

Why all this largess? Pure job politics. What we didn't know (and just lucked into) was that the mayor was up for reelection in four months and had promised in her previous campaign that she would attract 5,000 new jobs. She was 60 short of that goal with four months to go. You need to ask and to sell the fact that you are creating jobs.

☞ **HANDS ON:** Make sure you talk to your mayor's or county commissioner's office about the economic development funding and lending available. Check regularly, as these programs are always changing. And, make sure you know where the enterprise zones (or whatever your local name may be) are in your community. You'll feel pretty dumb if you expand your services into a building that you pay full rent or purchase price for when on the other side of the street you could get low- or no-interest financing because that's where the enterprise zone starts.

e. Mortgages. This type of debt is longer term and is limited to bricks and mortar. The terms of mortgages were traditionally 30 years, but now come in 5-, 10-, 12-, 15-, and 20-year terms, with fixed or variable interest, sometimes with a big payment (balloon) at the end. Like all kinds of borrowing, everything is negotiable, so be an informed buyer of money.

☞ **HANDS ON:** Most local newspapers publish a weekly summary of local mortgage (and certificate of deposit) rates in the business section or perhaps the real estate section. If that is not the case in your paper, call the chamber of commerce or the reference desk at your local library. They often also compile these comparative numbers.

3. Other Sources of Capital

While most banks and savings and loans offer some combination of the five traditional kinds of financing, there are a lot of other options in borrowing and in financing your new business or expansion. Remember that the idea is to lower or fund your cash needs. This doesn't necessarily require borrowing from the bank. Let's examine these different ways to fill your cash holes.

One of the first places to look is within your own organization. Are there different ways of handling areas of your not-for-profit that will free up additional capital and create a more effective operation? Do you have equity available in-house such as savings accounts or cash values in other assets that can be sold or used as collateral? If you still come up short, you may want to consider one of these financing techniques:

a. Lean on your suppliers. The people you buy from have a vested interest in your growth. If you have a well-written business plan, you can go to them and suggest, at least for the first few months, that you need longer credit terms. If you intend to establish a long-term relationship with a supplier in order to produce your product or service, maybe the supplier is willing to extend your credit line to help nurture your business relationship. Some suppliers may extend the payment period or agree to give you a loan for the materials at a reduced interest rate (usually 1 to 2 percent over the prime interest rate).

b. Purchase on consignment. If you can't afford inventory, try to arrange to purchase it on consignment. Payment isn't due until you sell it. In our community, several local artists create potpourri and herb products that are displayed and sold in a not-for-profit memorial garden gift shop. The materials the artists use come from the wildflower and herb areas of the gardens. By selling items on consignment, the not-for-profit keeps upfront cash costs at a minimum and pays for a product only when it sells.

c. Explore leasing needed equipment. By leasing equipment, you eliminate the upfront cash cost of down payments. Leasing may result in higher long-term costs, so shop around for leasing agreements and terms. Banks and lenders have information on leasing companies. And keep alert to changing deals. For example, several friends of mine always lease their cars and save significant money over owning. The catch? They don't really care what kind of car they drive. When they go to lease, they find a kind of car that is not selling well, that will often be leased by the car dealer to recover some money, if not the full purchase price. They then negotiate the lease, with a complete willingness to walk away. Over a three- or five-year lease term, they often save $4,000 to $9,000. So don't assume that leasing is always more expensive. Run the numbers.

d. Pay suppliers directly. This is one way to avoid raising money to pay suppliers for materials. Presell your product or service and get your customer to pay suppliers directly. In order for this to work, customers must *really* want your product. And you must be willing to put the deal together with suppliers.

The idea of these financing options is to reduce the cash flow out of your organization early in the business start-up phase when it is most vulnerable. Be creative, and stay informed about your options.

C. SOURCES OF FINANCING

Now that you are armed with knowledge about the kinds of debt you can go for, where are the places you can go to apply for a loan? Lending has gotten very competitive with deregulation, and there are a myriad of choices for you to consider. As you read through the following list, remember that not all lenders are equal and not all make sense for your organization. You need to match your business with your organization and your borrowing needs carefully. At the end of this chapter, we'll talk more about finding the right bank and how to appeal to lenders, but keep in mind as you go through this part of the chapter that we're just reviewing options.

1. Commercial Banks

These are the full-service firms that are increasingly big, increasingly national or international in scope, and have the initials *FDIC* painted on their doors. Banks offer the full gamut of services, including checking, savings, certificates of deposit, money market funds, payroll services, investment counseling, bill payment services, and, of course, a buffet of loans. Commercial banks are very, very competitive, and, although you may not have considered it, you have something they want.

☞ **HANDS ON:** Banks want your checking account. Why? Because that is the money they use to lend to other people and organizations. They take the funds you deposit and quickly loan them out to other people, paying you little or no interest, and charging a higher rate to their borrowers. This difference in interest is what makes the banks most of their money, along with the various and sundry fees that they love to tack on. Look at it this way. Take the total amount that you run through your checking account per year, and multiply it by 85 percent, which allows the banks to comply with the reserves that they need to keep on hand. Let's say you have a $2 million annual budget, and all of that goes through your organizational checking account at some point. Eighty-five percent of $2 million is $1.60 million. If you multiply that number by the current prime rate, you get a rough idea of how much the bank makes on your checking account each year. If the prime is 5.5 percent, the bank profits roughly $88,000 a year on your deposits! And you thought you had to beg for a loan! Remember, you are the customer, and you come with an attraction, your checking account, that most, if not all, banks will find extremely attractive.

For the same reasons, most banks will want you to establish a checking account if they become your major lender. This is not unreasonable, but it *is* negotiable. Keep that in mind as you shop.

2. Savings and Loans
Savings and loans are mostly locally chartered lending institutions. You can tell that they are a savings and loan by the fact that on their doors the initials *FSLIC* are visible. The vast majority of their lending is to private individuals for mortgages, but in the 1980s most savings and loans established commercial lending subsidiaries, particularly for commercial real estate. Check them out as lending options.

3. Credit Unions
Credit unions are cooperatives and exist for the benefit of their depositors. Credit unions lend to their membership, usually smaller loans for such things as vehicles and home improvement, but they also can be approached if your services will benefit their members.

❑ FOR EXAMPLE: A client organization of mine needed to buy vans to transport their disabled residents from group homes to work, shopping, church, and recreation events. A family member of one of the residents who was on the board of directors pointed out that the local Catholic Credit Union had lent money to the parochial schools for their activity buses, and perhaps would consider a loan to the agency. The staff checked on the religious affiliation of the residents and their families, finding that 74 percent were, in fact, Catholic. They approached the credit union, and in their application for funding noted that one of the purposes of the loan would be to transport residents to and from mass. They got the loan, at a very attractive rate.

4. Program-Related Investments (PRIs)

These kinds of loans come from foundations who, in the mid 1980s, discovered that lending to organizations often promoted a better outcome in the not-for-profit borrower than just a straight grant. If you are considering a new or expanded method of providing service, talk to a foundation that has interest in your project and ask if it does PRIs. Again, the loan rates can be very attractive, and PRIs are often used for start-up costs and working capital. I like PRIs for social entrepreneurs because they bring foundations into the entrepreneurial loop and force them to participate in the risk-reward cycle of the free market.

5. Tax-Exempt Bond Issuers

As a not-for-profit, you may have the ability to issue tax-exempt bonds, which are just loans that pay interest that is free from taxation for the lender. Since the interest is nontaxable, the amount you pay in interest can be much less. Many large sophisticated not-for-profits (colleges, hospitals, etc.) issue their own bonds, but it is an expensive and technically complex process. As a result, more and more state associations now offer bond pools, in which many not-for-profits come together to group their borrowing needs into one large issuance, so that they keep their costs of issuance down to a reasonable amount. Call your peers and your state trade association to find out if these are being offered or considered.

There are also a large number of quasigovernmental bond issuers (for parks, rehabilitated housing, airport districts, water districts, historic preservation, etc.) that are always looking for qualified participants to increase the size of their issues. Check around with your banker, realtor (if property is involved), and chamber of commerce to see who does this kind of financing in your community.

These are the main sources of loans that I recommend to you. I would suggest that you stay away from commercial lenders, who are almost always more expensive, and avoid private individuals as sources of capital. In both cases the price you pay will be way too high to be considered good stewardship.

D. RULES FOR FINANCING

Borrowing money is not something to be taken lightly, although I have said repeatedly that social entrepreneurs understand that it is often a worthwhile and essential part of the entire mission-based venture. At the same time, if you do decide you need to borrow, there are some rules that you can follow to keep your risk reasonable and to keep your costs affordable. I have offered up six rules for financing that have worked for my clients as well as for my own business and personal borrowing. Here they are:

1. *Never borrow unless you are making money, or unless your business plan shows that you will.* I know that I've already told you this twice, but I can't tell you it enough. There is no excuse for applying for a loan when you are losing money, or when you can't project that you will be making money in a short time. Your lender will almost certainly turn you down, and worse, you may well damage your reputation in the business community, something you can ill afford in today's more competitive mission-based arena.

2. *Everything is negotiable.* This, too, I have told you earlier in this chapter. And this, too, bears repeating. The bank is selling you money. You are the customer. Lending is a very competitive business. Banks want your money and, if you have a good business plan, want to sell you a loan. Nothing is final, not the interest rate, term, points, collateral, down payment, or other fees until you sign the documents.

❏ **FOR EXAMPLE:** In 1992, my business went sour, due to some things I probably should have foreseen, and a couple that no one but God could have predicted. I had 15 employees, a large line of credit, and some equipment loans still to pay off. I did what everyone should do when things turn sour, I developed a plan (which included some internal sacrifices, such as my not getting paid and some extensions of my loan payments). I then went to the bank, plan in hand. The bankers listened to my problems and considered my suggestions. They finally said, "Okay, we can live with your plan, but we need to add some more collateral. We want to have second position on your home." What that meant was that they could take my house if my business went down the tube. This was a nonstarter from my point of view. My position was pretty weak, since my business was on the critical list. But I said, "No way. You have all of my business assets as collateral, and they are more valuable than the sum of the loans I have outstanding to you. I'll report to you weekly for the next six months, if that will make you feel better, but you're not getting my house. Not a chance." And I held my breath. Their immediate answer, "Okay, we just had to ask. I'm sure you understand." And the loan extensions went through, the business recovered, and I never had to risk my house. Everything is negotiable.

3. *Expect to contribute some down payment and collateral.* Even though everything is negotiable, you have to be reasonable in your demands. It is reasonable for the lender to want your organization to contribute two things to a lending deal: a down payment and collateral. The amount and the terms of these items are negotiable, but don't whine about the fact of their being included.

4. *Always borrow for as short a term as possible.* The saying that time is money is really true about lending terms. The longer your loan is for, the more interest you will incur. It makes sense of course; you have the banker's money for a longer time. However, it is anything but a straight line increase. In other words, if you have the money twice as long, you don't pay twice the interest; you pay a whole lot more. And that is why I urge you to borrow for as short a term as possible.

❏ **FOR EXAMPLE:** Look at the difference in monthly payments and total interest on a $100,000 mortgage at 7 percent with a 15-year repayment as opposed to a 30-year repayment.

Principal: $100,000

Interest Rate: 7%

	15 years	30 years
Monthly payment	$898.83	$665.30
Total interest	$61,789.00	$139,508.00

By paying $233.53 more each month—or $42,034 over a 15-year period—the borrower saves $77,719 in interest! Again, run the numbers on a variety of options and always be sure to calculate the entire interest cost.

5. *Always seek a variable-rate, fixed-payment loan.* This one is going to take some explaining, so hang in there with me. First the *variable rate.* Variable-rate loans nearly always start at a lower interest rate than fixed-rate ones do. This is because as overall rates (and, thus, the bank's cost of money) change, the bank adjusts your rate and always continues to make the same difference in interest costs. So, the bank has less risk, and lower risk for the bank means lower rates for you, at least to a point. So, a variable rate is better in terms of costs, but I know that having one of these also gives you fits in terms of worry about cash flow. What if rates sky-

rocket? How can you afford to take the risk? This is where the fixed-payment loan comes in. This type of loan also almost always has lower initial interest rates and allows you to plan your cash flows more accurately. If interest rates rise, your loan lengthens. If interest rates drop, the length of the loan decreases. And here's the secret: *In either case, your loan payment stays the same.* Thus, you can take advantage of the variable-rate loan and still sleep at night. These loans are very, very popular, for reasons I'm sure you can appreciate.

☞ **HANDS ON:** All variable-rate loans have a ceiling and a floor for their rates and a step rate. What this means is that if your loan starts at, say, 6 percent, it can go up no more than ½ percentage point a year, and down no more than ¼ point, with a top rate of perhaps 9 percent and a floor of 4.25 percent. While these are just examples, you get the idea. If you don't believe my admonition about the variable-rate, fixed-payment loan, run the numbers. Set up a spreadsheet to start you with a 20-year fixed-rate loan, put in the interest, principal, and the total payments. Then set up the variable-rate, fixed-payment loan. You'll start with a lower rate, but build in the worst case: Make the interest rate go up as soon as the loan allows and stay high for the remainder of the loan. You'll still pay less with the variable-rate fixed-payment loan. If you don't, call me, and I'll borrow from your bank!

6. *Always negotiate for the ability to prepay the loan at no penalty.* Paying a little extra each month on the principal significantly reduces your overall interest costs. The rule on a 30-year loan is that, if you pay twice the principal payment each month (which, as you know is very, very small in the first few years) you can cut the loan in half, and the total interest cost by two-thirds. So, particularly in those first months and years, add a bit to each payment. One way to do it is to budget for a round loan payment. For example, if your payment according to the loan documents is $654.45, budget and pay $700 a month from the start. If you use a computer-based check-writing program, just put $700 a month in, and don't think about it any more. You will be amazed at how much faster you pay off the loan.

These six rules will really lower your costs and lower your risks when you do borrow for your entrepreneurial activities.

E. DEALING WITH LENDERS

In this section, we'll deal with the last link in the lending chain, the lenders themselves. You need to understand how lenders think and, more importantly, how they think of not-for-profits. The most important opinion, of course, is how *your* lender thinks of *your* organization, and by the end of this section, you should have an excellent handle on how to secure a great opinion from an appropriate lender.

1. How Lenders Think

The most important thing for you to know as you seek to work with any group of people is how they think and what their perspective is on your relationship. This understanding allows you to see your interactions through their eyes, and while you may well not share their perspective, at least you know why they feel and act the way they do. This is certainly true for lenders and for your relationship with them.

Lenders abhor one thing above all others—risk. Risk is their ultimate four-letter word. The risk they are concerned about is the risk of not getting paid back by their borrowers. Risk comes in lots of forms, a bad economy, an imprudent borrower, a poor local business market. Risks can be real and can be perceived, but if the lender perceives a risk, for the borrower, it might as well be real.

For borrowers, risk translates into higher interest rates, higher starting interest points, more down payment, more collateral, a shorter loan term, or even no loan at all. So, the more risky a lender thinks you are, the more expensive it is. The less risky your organization is perceived, the cheaper it will be to buy some money when you need it. This is why people who are wealthy get cheap loans and have lenders falling all over themselves to provide loans and lines of credit: someone with high net assets and a strong cash flow is a low risk. Another good example of risk and lenders are the nearly ubiquitous offers of credit cards that come in the mail. You know the ones: "You have been preapproved for an XYZ Bank Gold Card. Your excellent credit has allowed us to set your initial borrowing limit at $5,000." How can the banks do that with a group of strangers? Well, they do check the credit records—which are public—and that reduces some of their risk. And then, of course, they charge you 18, 20, or even 21 percent annual interest, which covers a whole lot of risk.

So, risk is the big no-no for lenders. And their desire to maximize profits and minimize risk is both understandable and very capitalistic in outlook. Don't forget, as a social entrepreneur, you want to maximize mission and minimize risk. So, your motivations and the lenders' are closer than you may think.

2. How Lenders See Not-for-Profits

How do lenders see most not-for-profits? Seven letters. Capitalized. Underlined. Bold face. Twenty-four-point type.

BAD RISK

Why? Look at it from their perspective. You are, after all a *non*-profit, meaning to them (as it does to most of your community) that you lose money. If you lose money, how can you pay back their loan? And they know that many, many 501(c)(3)s operate as charities rather than not-for-profit businesses. They may well have sat on the board of directors of one of your local charitable peers, and others may be customers of their banks. If they have not-for-profit customers, they almost certainly have been approached by one or more of those organizations for a loan, usually when the organization is at its lowest ebb, losing money hand over fist.

As a result, they generalize that all not-for-profits are poorly run, poorly managed, and not at all a good risk. And that perspective, that prejudice, is what you have to overcome. But first, you have to find the best bank for your organization.

3. Seeking the Best Lender for Your Organization

I am a strong believer that one of your key entrepreneurial relationships is with your banker. You need this person to be part of your social entrepreneur team, if not actually on the committee, certainly on board with the idea, and well informed of your plans and progress. Not all banks, however, are set up to embrace entrepreneurs of any stripe, much less social entrepreneurs.

It is important to understand that banks have target markets, just like any well-run business. Some focus on import-export, some on Fortune 1000 firms, some on technology, some on real estate, some on individual customers, some on small business, and the last one is the bank you want. The small business mindset, whether for-profit or not-for-profit is the expertise you should seek. How do you do that? After all, if you ask any bankers if they want small business customers, they will all answer, "Of course!" But you can search out their true priorities a different way.

☞ **HANDS ON:** I am sure that you know someone who knows the CEO (or branch manager) of one of your local full-service banks. In fact, if you list three banks, you probably have a network that gets you in contact with the top person at all three. Ask that someone to call his or her friend the banker, letting the banker know that your organization is looking for a new bank. Make sure you mention your annual budget size. The conversation between your friend, who we'll call Al, and his friend, the bank CEO, who we'll call Cheryl, goes like this:

AL: Hi, Cheryl, how's the family?
CHERYL: Fine, Al, what can I do for you?

AL: I just wanted to give you a heads-up. You know the local children's museum? Well, I know the exec, and he just told me that they are looking around for a new bank. He told me that their annual budget is over $2.4 million. Just thought you might like the tip on the business.

CHERYL: Thanks, Al. We'll follow up.

AL: Okay, have a good day.

Now, what has Al done? He's done you a favor and Cheryl a favor, while making no promises about your credit or business skills.

Now comes the fun part. Once you have done this at two or three banks, you wait for a call, and see who makes it. Is it the CEO? A junior loan accountant who has been on board two weeks? The bank that wants you, that values small business will be the one that calls back, and the person who calls will be higher ranking. This method is very, very accurate in finding banks that really want to work with you and value you as a customer.

☞ **HANDS ON:** When you actually do go visit the bank of your choice, ask a lot of questions, and remember, the bank wants your checking deposits. You are the customer. Don't go in with an attitude that the bank is doing you a favor by letting you open a checking account with it. Your checking account is an asset. How much can you squeeze out of it in services? Finally, even if you don't decide to change banks, go to your current bank and let it know you are looking around. You'll be amazed at the offers of services that drop out of the sky.

❑ **FOR EXAMPLE:** Here's a fabulous idea that a client of mine used on its bank. Most personal checking accounts that fall below a certain minimum average balance are subject to a monthly fee. Since most of this organization's staff were low-paid workers, their accounts were all being assessed this fee, which was big money to them. The agency went to its bank when it was considering other banks, and asked whether, for keeping the agency deposits with the bank, the bank would waive the monthly fee for all of the agency's employees. The bank immediately agreed. What a win-win! The agency had just negotiated a no-cost fringe benefit, and the bank had an incentive with which to attract new customers.

Once you find the right bank, stay there. You don't want to be changing banks every year or two. The development of a long-term mutually beneficial relationship is crucial. And that is the subject of our next section.

4. Developing and Maintaining a Good Relationship with Your Banker

Now that you have the right bank, how do you maximize the relationship and get the most from your bank and banker? By investing time and attention. Why do you want to make that effort? Because banking is still really a personal business. Whether the bank lends you money or not depends in large part on how your banker sees you and your management team as individuals. You need the banker to see you and your management team as good businesspeople, and to do that you have to overcome bankers' prejudice against not-for-profits in general. The banker can also help you in your cash and capital planning, give you great ideas on your strategic and business plans, be a resource for local economic development funding, and be a key part of your local business networking.

Additionally, it is important to remember that when you do apply for a loan, your banker is your advocate. He or she will present your loan to a loan committee whose job it is to minimize the bank's risk. All of the other members of the loan committee have the prejudice against not-for-profits that I discussed earlier, and you can't even go into the committee meeting. It is up to your banker to overcome the prejudice as well as peer pressure. Before the meeting, you better work on the banker's opinion of you. Here's how.

a. Keep your banker informed. Lack of information translates directly into more risk in a lender's mind. Send your banker your monthly income and expense statements, your audits, your newsletter, your letters of accreditation award, and news stories (hopefully good ones) about your organization. Keep your organization's name and logo on the banker's desk by regular incoming mail.

b. Meet with your banker on a regular basis. Meet with your banker twice a year, once when your audit is complete and six months later. This meeting should be all business. Talk income and expense, staff turnover, what the newest bill in Congress or the state legislature means to you. Toss out occupancy, or new admissions, or new donor numbers, in other words, talk business talk, not mission. Let the banker see the social entrepreneur, not the charitable administrator. Go over your financial projections for the next six months as well, and talk about any future financing needs you see, even a year or two in advance.

c. Get your banker out of the bank. Invite the banker to see what you do where you do it, at least once a year. Also invite the banker to open houses or dedications of new buildings. Some of my clients invite their bankers to be observers at their boards' meetings to discuss the next year's budget. You want the banker to see what you do, and how well you do it.

☞ **HANDS ON:** Think of these visits as inspections, which in a very real sense, they are. Make sure your staff know that the banker is coming, and that they are on their best behavior. Make sure the lawn is mowed, the building is clean, and so forth. Put your best foot forward. The impressions your banker takes back will go a long way toward his or her opinion of your organization and of you as a manager.

The relationship with your lender is a crucial one. Even though these three steps may sound like a lot of work, they really aren't, and they certainly are a good investment of your time in terms of the benefits your organization gets back.

RECAP

In this chapter, you learned about your choices in financing techniques. First, you heard about the prime rule of borrowing, which is this: *Only borrow if you are making money, or if your business plan projects a profit.* This one rule is the most important of all and is often very difficult for new social entrepreneurs to understand.

Then we turned to ways that you can assess your borrowing needs. We looked at forms that can help you assess your capital costs, start-up expenses, and working capital needs. These allow you to get the best feel on how much to plan to borrow.

Third, we looked at the many different methods of financing, going through the various kinds of debt instruments that are available. After this, we looked at the many sources of financing, including banks, savings and loans, suppliers, and other less common lenders. Then we turned our attention to rules for borrowing, which include not only my preeminent decree on making money but the standards of borrowing for the shortest term possible at a variable rate, with a fixed payment. And, remember that everything in the borrowing process is negotiable!

Finally, we looked at how to work with your lender, getting the most out of the organization as possible, and I provided you with some tips on finding the right bank.

Financing is a nerve-wracking issue for some, almost a natural thing for others. Whichever category you fall in, remember that finance is one of the technical things that social entrepreneurs need to be fluent in to do their jobs well.

Speaking of technicalities, that is certainly the issue in our next chapter on the Unrelated Business Income Tax and corporate structures.

QUESTIONS FOR DISCUSSION: CHAPTER 9

1. In light of Peter's rules, should we revisit our current borrowing patterns?

2. Do we need a line of credit? For how much?

3. Should we consider changing banks? Why or why not?

4. Are we getting appropriate terms from our suppliers now? Are there ways of improving them?

5. How can we improve our relations with our lenders? Who should be the primary contact?

10

Technicalities: Unrelated Business Income Tax and Corporate Structuring

OVERVIEW

In this chapter you will learn about the following:

➤ The Unrelated Business Income Tax
➤ Uses of Corporate structuring in Social Entrepreneurship

Social entrepreneurs unfortunately must, like the rest of us, deal with technicalities. While the concept of innovation in pursuit of mission is a strategic one, the day-to-day implementation of the strategy can become completely stagnated if the technical details are not attended to. Some of these details show up in marketing, some in finance, some in customer service, and some in this chapter. Here, we will deal with two very misunderstood parts of the not-for-profit business cycle: the Unrelated Business Income Tax (UBIT) and corporate structures. To risk generalization, the first is overfeared, and the second is overused. Both are much misunderstood, with poor, if not outright false, information too often coming from advisors such as attorneys and accountants which muddy the waters considerably. In this chapter, I'll first tell you the facts of the UBIT and corporate structure options, and then show you how you can use the knowledge to both benefit your mission and keep your organizational nose clean.

Make no mistake: Not paying attention to the UBIT rules can get you in real trouble. Disregard the tax code at your own and your organization's peril. The same is true for corporate restructuring. Not only are there legal and tax issues to attend to, the very fact of developing more than one corporation can and often does draw attention, scrutiny, and sometimes disapproval from key funders or regulators.

As with everything else in the social entrepreneur's world, the axis around which both issues revolve is your organization's mission. For UBIT, the exact language of your charitable purpose will decide whether you have a tax liability. In corporate structuring, you need to be able to show a valid mission purpose to justify the expense of the additional corporations. Yet again, your mission should lead you.

A. THE UNRELATED BUSINESS INCOME TAX

Let me be clear from the start. The Unrelated Business Income Tax is a good thing, a fair tax, one that you, as a not-for-profit manager, want on the record. Why? Because unlike so much other tax manipulation, UBIT does what it set out to: It levels the playing field and gives your organization some protection against assaults on you from businesses believing that you have an unfair (untaxed) advantage.

At its core, UBIT says this: *If your organization makes a profit from activities not included in your mission statement, your organization, like any other, should pay a tax on those profits.* That's it. Pretty simple and straightforward. Unfortunately, a lot of people mistakenly attribute some pretty bad outcomes to UBIT. And I've heard dozens of half-truths or total fabrications about UBIT in my consultations with social entrepreneurs. So, let me address what UBIT *doesn't* do, here and now.

UBIT *doesn't* say that your organization loses its tax-exempt 501(c)(3) status if it is subject to taxation. UBIT *doesn't* tax all your income, not even all your unrelated income, just your unrelated profits. It *doesn't* cause you to lose your ability to accept donations or government or foundation contracts. UBIT is not the end of the world.

But UBIT *is* part of the tax code, and you *do* need to pay close attention to it. If you are subject to any part of the UBIT, for a new or an existing part of your services, you need to file notice with the Internal Revenue Service (IRS) annually with form 990-T. Just because UBIT is not Armageddon does not mean you can ignore it.

1. The Definition of Unrelated and Related

With that as introduction, let's look at the IRS rules themselves and try to sort out what you, your SE team, and your board need to know about this issue. Definitions first. The entire issue of UBIT has to do with whether your new or expanded service is related to your mission statement. The IRS defines relatedness as follows:

A *related* (*nontaxable*) *service* is one that makes important contributions to the charitable purpose of your organization, regardless of how large or small that business venture is.

An *unrelated (taxable) service* does not importantly contribute to your organization's charitable purpose.

As I said earlier, it all revolves around the wording of your organization's mission statement.

❏ **FOR EXAMPLE:** An organization that works with chronically mentally ill individuals was willed a fast-food restaurant, one that had annual income of $1.5 million and a profit of $150,000. The mission statement of the center read, "Rehabilitate and train for competitive employment people with mental illness as their primary diagnosis." Nothing in there about flipping burgers; thus, the net income was Unrelated Business Income. The profits ($150,000) were taxable. The organization paid $41,750 in taxes ($150,000 times the current taxable rates) and retained the rest, some of which was invested back in the restaurant, some of which went to mission purposes.

The next year, the center decided to use the restaurant as a place to train people with mental illness to work in the fast-food industry. Look at the mission statement: ". . . train for competitive employment . . ." Bingo! The income was suddenly related to the mission, and all of the $150,000 profits stayed in the organization. But *then,* the IRS found that the organization was employing people with mental illness for years at a time, and in the opinion of the IRS, this was not "training for competitive employment." Oops. Suddenly the income was unrelated again, and taxes on the profits were due.

As you can see, wording is everything in deciding whether your income is subject to UBIT. And, in the preceding definition of *related* and *unrelated,* the term *important contribution* is subjective and vague. So, the IRS makes the issue somewhat clearer by adding a set of more (but not completely) quantifiable criteria.

1. *Is this business venture a trade or business?*   This criterion is to check and see whether what you are doing is considered in the commercial world a trade or business. Thus, our fast-food restaurant would be, since there are many for-profit fast-food places. In today's world, there are not too many examples of activities that are not commercialized, but a ministry would be one.

2. *Is the business regularly carried out with the frequency of a like commercial venture?*   This criterion checks to make sure that the business is open according to standard business hours for that industry. This provision is here to protect once-a-year charity auctions,

annual charity golf outings, and, specifically, the sale of Girl Scout cookies, all of which have private sector competition.

3. *Is it unrelated to our tax-exempt organization's mission and purpose?* This question has three subsets, the first of which is pretty subjective, a yes answer to all three is needed to be able to answer question 3 "no."

   a. *Does it significantly contribute to our organization's mission?* Absolutely the most subjective item in the list.

   b. *Is the scope of our business venture appropriate? Is the business operating this business outside the geographic boundaries stated in the bylaws? Is the size of the business activity appropriate?* If you have geographic or demographic exclusions in your mission statement, you can get hurt under this or the next criterion. For example, if you list a specific set of counties you serve in your mission, and you now get funds for working in an additional location, you may be subject to UBIT.

   c. *Is the beneficiary class appropriate?* This is the same issue as in criterion b, except dealing with the kinds of people you serve. Thus, if your mission statement says that your mission is to serve senior citizens and you start a family preservation center that serves people younger than 50 or 55, you may have unrelated income.

If your answer is yes to questions 1, 2, and 3, the venture is *probably an unrelated business.* And, that means you have to do some specific reporting and accounting of your unrelated income and the associated expenses, which we'll cover more in a few pages. Be sure to consult your articles of incorporation, bylaws, or constitution to determine what your charitable purpose is and in what areas you operate. If it is out of date, revise it to bring it into compliance with the reality of your organization, and file the amended mission statement with the IRS (or Revenue Canada for Canadian readers).

2. Exceptions to the IRS Rules

There are, of course, exceptions to the UBIT rules. These are as follows, as of this writing:

A business primarily staffed by volunteers (85:15 ratio). An example of this would be a thrift store or gift shop that is staffed by volunteers.

If the goods sold by your not-for-profit are donated, paid staff can be involved in the business venture. The Salvation Army's sale of donated items is an excellent example.

Passive income from the following sources is *usually* considered related for not-for-profit organizations: dividends, interest, some rent, capital gains and losses, and other similar items—unless the dividends come from controlled for-profit subsidiaries.

Sales resulting from a convenience (such as a cafeteria, bookstore, or parking lot) for staff, visitors, or clients. If used by the public, unrelated business income may apply.

Now, let's look at some examples of what has recently been found to have been unrelated (and thus potentially taxable) income:

- All net advertising income, unless the sale is carried on irregularly. This is why there is such an increase in sponsorships for events. See any public broadcasting show for guidance on what is acceptable.
- Sale of your organization's name.
- Providing services such as management, billing, technical assistance, or administrative support to other not-for-profits.
- Renting facilities or equipment to other not-for-profits is iffy. If the equipment or building was purchased with debt, the income is unrelated. If not, it *may* be unrelated.

3. A Profit Tax, Not an Income Tax

Here is the central issue that is the most misunderstood about UBIT: Although the name of the regulation is the Unrelated Business *Income* Tax, the term *income* to the IRS means *profits* to you and me. What the law does is put you on the same plane with for-profit organizations. For-profits pay a portion of their *profits* in taxes, not a percentage of their income. This is often confusing for not-for-profit staff who only pay personal income taxes, which are based on a percentage of income. But the issue for your organization is to remember that for any amount of unrelated income, there is an amount, perhaps smaller, perhaps larger, of unrelated *expense*. Thus, just because you have unrelated income doesn't mean you will automatically pay taxes.

❏ FOR EXAMPLE: A number of years ago, an organization came to me to discuss its concern about an internal finding that it had unrelated income from a service business that it had started. The organization's mission was to do environmental preservation, and it did the fairly standard mix of community awareness education, lobbying at the local and county level, and watchdog duty to attempt to keep its community near the Pacific coast relatively pristine. With over 25 years of history, this organization had developed a large group of supporters, some who donated money, some time, some who served on the board, and some who just subscribed to and read the newsletter. In the course of its watchdog work surrounding waste dumping from local manufacturers, the organization had developed the capability to test ground- and runoff water for toxic materials. It had received a grant, hired technically proficient staff, and bought the appropriate equipment. Its efforts at uncovering spills had wound up in the newspaper and on television, and soon a few of the organization's newsletter subscribers asked the staff to test the subscribers' own groundwater, just to be sure that there was nothing amiss. The subscribers weren't near a factory, nor were they downstream from a power plant; they just wanted to know what, if anything, was in their water, and went to the expert, the not-for-profit organization. The staff agreed to come out, but for a fee.

You can guess the rest. The organization did more and more farm and home water testing, and began to develop significant income (over $50,000 per year) from this work. Then one day its corporate attorney called and said that she was pretty sure that income from the water testing was unrelated income subject to UBIT. The management team went a little nuts with nightmares about high taxes and, since one of them had been to a training session of mine on business development, they called me. The conversation went like this:

ME: Let's start with the worst possible case, and assume that you are, in fact, subject to UBIT for this income. How much income did you have from water testing last year?

THEM: Nearly $54,500.

ME: And what were the water-testing expenses?

THEM: What?

ME: How much did you spend on travel, staff, depreciation on equipment, supplies, overhead, support staff, employee benefits, and the like to support the part of the water-testing efforts for which you were paid by farmers and homeowners?

THEM: Haven't a clue.

ME: Ah. Okay, why don't you sit down with your accountant and figure all of that out. Be careful to include every legitimate cost. Then fax me the results, and we'll talk again.

THEM: Okay, we'll get on it.

Three days later my fax machine beeped and out came the results of their accounting: The total expenses for home and farm water testing were just under $60,000, $59,740 to be exact. I called the management team back:

ME: Thanks for the information. There's good news and bad news. . . .

THEM: Start with the good news.

ME: On the assumption that your numbers are accurate, you don't owe any taxes to the feds for last year.

THEM: That is good. And the bad?

ME: You don't owe any money because the "business" had a loss. UBIT is a tax on profits, and you didn't have any. In fact, you lost $5,340 on this work last year. That's almost 10 percent of revenue. It's not a fund-raiser for you, that's for sure. In the future, I sure would look at raising your prices, and at least trying to break even. Remember, if you *do* make money, you need to pay taxes at normal business rates. But paying taxes is a *good* problem, because it *means you are making money,* and you'll have some left over after the feds take their piece.

So don't go berserk when you think you have a UBIT issue. Every dollar of unrelated income has some amount (in the preceding case, about $1.10!) of unrelated expenses. If your venture is making money, you owe taxes. If it isn't, you don't, but you might want to rethink your pricing structure!

4. Deciding Whether Your Business Is Subject to UBIT

As you can see, there is a lot of technical expertise needed to really nail down your UBIT status if you find you are in a gray area. And that brings up a question: How can you really tell whether you are subject to this tax? You can look at similar situations, but the IRS does not lean on precedent as much as most state or federal courts. That means that while a similar situation can give you guidance, it will not provide you with absolute assurance that you are not falling under the UBIT rules.

The only way to absolutely, finally, tell whether you are subject to UBIT is to ask the IRS for what it calls a Private Letter Ruling (PLR). PLRs are very expensive to file (often between $5,000 and $10,000 in legal and accounting fees), and it takes anywhere from five to 15 months to receive an answer from the IRS. The problems here are multiple. First, obviously, is the expense. But for many organizations that are starting up a new service, an equally troubling issue is the delay. The new ventures that your SE team will come up with will almost certainly be focused on providing mission: That is your core competency. An idea to do mission will be based on an unmet or poorly met need in your community. A delay to wait for an IRS ruling will delay meeting that need, and your community will suffer as a result.

But, your board, and perhaps your funders may well want assurance that you are not subject to UBIT. So what do you do? Think about this route. I usually recommend that my clients who are unsure of their UBIT status not go after a PLR before starting up services for a reason that may surprise you: For most new businesses, *it is easier, quicker, cheaper, and less controversial to assume your income is unrelated and thus taxable.* Surprised? I thought you would be. But let's look at an example of why this makes sense from a mission, money, and strategic perspective.

Using the information in Exhibit 10-1, let's play out a scenario where, in one option, you wait to start a venture until you have a PLR, and in the other, you go ahead and provide services immediately, assuming your venture is taxable. A *unit of service* is just that, perhaps one day of education, one office visit, one immunization, whatever the organization does. In option 1, your PLR decides you are taxable and is returned quickly enough to let you start the venture in year two—a record pace. In both options, once the service is started the income and expenses are identical.

Here you see that the venture, not unusually, lost money its first two years and made a small surplus in its third. But because the IRS allows you to carry forward past losses, you wouldn't have to pay taxes until at least

Exhibit 10-1   To wait or not to wait.

Option 1: Wait for PLR	Year 1	Year 2	Year 3	3 Year Total
Service provided	0	250 units	500 units	**750 units**
Legal expenses	$7,500	0	0	**$7,500**
Income from venture	$0	$5,000	$10,000	**$15,000**
Expenses from venture	$0	$7,000	$12,500	**$19,500**
Net income (loss) including legal fees	$0	($2,000)	($2,500)	**($12,000)**
UBIT taxes paid	$0	$0	$0	**$0**
Option 2: Go ahead with the assumption of UBIT				
Service provided	250 units	500 units	1,250 units	**2,000 units**
Legal expenses	$0	$0	$0	**$0**
Income from venture	$5,000	$10,000	$25,000	**$40,000**
Expenses from venture	$7,000	$12,500	$21,400	**$40,900**
Net income (loss)	($2,000)	($2,500)	$3,600	**($900)**
Carryforward from prior years	NA	($2,000)	($4,500)	
UBIT taxes paid	$0	$0	$0	**$0**

year four. *And,* you have no legal expense up front. *And,* you get services to the public sooner. Obviously, you need to run your own numbers and make sure that this idea makes sense for you. But in my experience, in many cases, it will!

5. A Decision Checklist for the Unrelated Business Income Tax

To make this a bit simpler, I've developed the matrix in Exhibit 10-2. *Note:* This is not an IRS-approved diagram! It is designed to help you weave your way through this potential problem, but will give you no shelter in case the IRS comes calling.

Now, if you determine that one or more of your ventures is unrelated to your organization's charitable purpose and the business earns a profit, *pay the taxes!* If a not-for-profit earns over $1,500 a year in profit from an unrelated venture, the organization must file a separate IRS tax return called a 990T Business Tax Return *and* pay taxes based on the current corporate rates. The current corporate rates can be found at the IRS Web site. The rates, as of this writing, are shown in Exhibit 10-3.

It is whole lot better to pay the tax than to risk a penalty from the IRS. It makes no sense to scrap a business venture that can earn additional income for your agency because the agency may have to pay tax on the profits. Look at this in another way. If a venture earns a net profit (after expenses) of $25,000 and the tax is paid at the present corporate rate of 15 percent, a not-for-profit will earn $21,250 in additional income. So, think of paying taxes as a good problem, and remember: Paying taxes does not threaten your organization's not-for-profit status, but *not* paying taxes does threaten *your* legal status—you may go to jail, pay a fine, or both!

In closing on this section, let me reiterate that UBIT is an important thing to pay attention to, but it is certainly not the easiest subject for a fledgling social entrepreneur to grasp. You can't just blow it off and ignore it. The concept is fair for everyone, so take the time to study the issue, and get help from your attorney and/or CPA. You don't want to risk your organizational status because you didn't do your homework. That's not what I mean when I talk about taking reasonable risk!

B. USES OF CORPORATE STRUCTURING IN SOCIAL ENTREPRENEURSHIP

On to corporate structures, the second technical issue in this chapter. In general, corporate structuring is overused, overrated, and misunderstood, and in the last category, it shares much with UBIT. But corporate struc-

Exhibit 10-2 A decision matrix for UBIT.

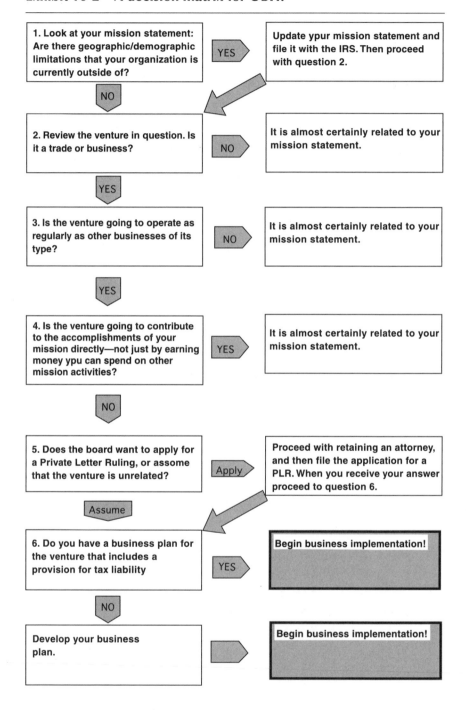

Exhibit 10-3   Corporate federal tax rates—January 2000.

Taxable Income	Tax Rate
First $1,500 (tax-exempt)	0%
Under $50,000	15%
$50,000–$75,000	$7,500 + 25% of amount over $50,000
$75,000–$100,000	$13,750 + 34% of amount over $75,000
$100,000–$335,000	$22,250 + 39% of amount over $100,00
$335,000–$10,000,000	$113,900 + 34% of amount over $335,000

tures are also very, very effective tools that can be used to strengthen your organization, protect valuable resources, facilitate collaboration with other mission-based organizations, allow you to tap new financial resources, and, in certain situations, prevent the loss of your tax-exempt status.

Notice that in my description of corporate structures I used the term *tools.* I want to expand on that description here, as a caution to you. Corporate structures *are* tools, ones that are *very specialized,* to be used only in special circumstances and for special reasons. They are not panaceas for any ill your organization may suffer, although I see an awful lot of people who use them in just such a manner.

❏ **FOR EXAMPLE:** A specialized tool, while wonderful for a specialized task, has little or no value for other tasks and, in fact, may actually produce a counterproductive result. Think of the task of joining two pieces of wood together. You can use nails or screws. The former is usually faster and, for most situations, works fine. But screws tend to hold the joint longer, particularly if it will be under stress, and they allow dismantling if needed. Screws are better for most fine work or in harder wood, as long as you predrill a hole for the screw. Two different tools, two different uses. Now, let's look at the tools you use to nail or screw: the hammer and the screwdriver. Also special tools for special situations. If you try to nail in the nail with the screwdriver, well, not much happens. The screwdriver is not designed for that task. If you try to drive the screw with the hammer, the screw *will* go in, and quickly, and the job will *appear* to be done. But, by using a hammer instead of a screwdriver, you tear out the wood that holds the screw in place, and there is no strength in the joint at all. You need to use the right tool for the job.

And here's the secret: For most organizational jobs, the right tool is your existing not-for-profit structure. Most ventures that you will undertake will be easily housed in your current not-for-profit. Expansions of most activities will also usually be able to remain in your 501(c)(3). But there will be times when you need another tool, and in this chapter, I'll show you the uses, and abuses, of a number of different corporate configurations, including a second not-for-profit, a for-profit subsidiary, a cooperative, and a design for an umbrella corporation with many subsidiaries. But remember that the most common abuse of corporate restructuring is overuse.

Can new corporate structures help your organization as it pursues social entrepreneurism? Certainly. But, just as with any other action, you need to ask the following questions: Is the risk worth the reward? Does this investment make my organization more mission-capable? How? Why?

1. Rules for Corporate Structures

First things first. I have some primary rules for social entrepreneurs considering the use of corporate restructuring:

a. Keep it simple.

b. Document everything.

c. Keep time sheets for anyone who is working for more than one corporation.

Let's look at each of these in a little more detail.

a. Keep it simple. This is the preeminent rule for mission-based management. Additional corporations are expensive, and, in many cases complex. They can distract you from pursuing your core mission rather than increasing your organization's mission capability. So, the question you should first ask is not, "What additional corporations do I need?" to accomplish a particular goal, but rather, "Can I do this within my existing 501 (c)(3) structure?" Most of the time, the answer will be yes. If it is not, then try to keep it simple by establishing a second corporation that is just like your existing one: a not-for-profit. Only as a last resort should you turn to the specialized (and complex) tools of a for-profit, co-op, partnership, or umbrella corporate structure. I know that this may sound boring and a bit vanilla to many readers, but it is valid advice if your quest is to do the most mission for the money.

☞ **HANDS ON:** Here are some of the many bogus reasons I have heard over the years for establishing a new corporation. In *every* case, the organization eventually stayed with its one and only not-for-profit organization.

We are going to have a for-profit business.

We are going to have a business that will have unrelated income.

We are going to have a catalog.

We are starting a venture that will use a different name.

We want to start an endowment and call it a foundation.

We want to do business in a different city (or building, or county, or state, or country).

We are going to own stock in a for-profit business with which we will partner.

Let me repeat, *none* of these actions are, on their own, adequate reasons to establish an additional entity.

b. Document everything. If you do need to expand your number of corporations, you need to establish a superb record-keeping system, and do it right at the beginning. You must have written documentation on why you established this new entity (what the mission-based rationale was), who voted for and against it on the board, what the relationship between the new corporation and your existing one is, minutes of all board and committee meetings, bylaws, contracts between your existing not-for-profit and its new cousins including leases, management contacts, loans, and the like. Such contracts need to be legal documents really signed by two different people who can obligate their respective corporations. And, of course, you need excellent financial records, in most cases including an annual audit.

Why all this killing of trees? Because at some point, someone will come and ask why you need another corporation. That person will be a donor (Why do you need my donation since you have a for-profit subsidiary?), a funder (It looks like you are trying to hide resources from us!), a staff person (Why do we need to spend all this time and money on this?), or the press (It seems you are more interested in building a corporate kingdom instead of doing your mission. Are you hiding something? Any comments?). Even with all of the corporate structuring around, there are still many people who are suspicious when things they don't understand occur. And, corporate structures and their rationales are, at best, arcane, if not downright confusing on the surface. So, document, document, document.

c. Keep time sheets. I know, I know, you hate this. So does everyone else, but it's part of the cost of an additional corporation *if, and only if, you have any people who are working for more than one corporation and money is changing hands as a result.*

❏ **For Example:** In the early 1980s my health-planning organization set up an additional not-for-profit to do management consulting to other health-related not-for-profits in our 18-county service area in central Illinois. I was executive director of both organizations, and spent time in both. My "home" organization, the Health Systems Agency (HSA), billed the second organization for my time, as it did for a number of our other HSA staff. Because the HSA's federal funding was based on total budgeted expenses (including staff salaries) we had to account for all of our time, and *reduce our grant* by the hours we spent working for the second corporation. If we hadn't kept time sheets, we never would have been able to document the correct breakout of our staff time and would either have over- or underestimated it.

☞ **HANDS ON:** If you have any staff who "sell" time to another entity, they have to keep accurate track, by hour, of how much time they spend for that entity. It will allow you to bill accurately and to document and justify your staff expenses to other funders. Don't skimp on this kind of documentation.

Okay, enough with the cautionary tales and the rules. Let's look at the tools themselves, and why you would and would not use them.

2. A Second Not-for-Profit

This is the most common second corporation and, as I said earlier, the one I want you to consider first if you feel certain you need to add an entity to your corporate family. Common uses for a second not-for-profit include a foundation, a property-holding corporation to maximize income, and a separation of net income to avoid grant reductions. We'll examine the generic model first, and then look at some case studies of the common uses.

a. A generic not-for-profit model. Look at Exhibit 10-4. Your not-for-profit can set up a second not-for-profit and have some control over what goes on in NFP 2 through representation on NFP 2's board of directors and shared management. However, in most states, your not-for-profit must maintain an "arm's-length" uncontrolled relationship between the two corporations. This is required if any government or foundation funding goes from one entity to another, which is almost always the case. Thus, your organization *cannot* control a *majority* of the second NFP's board of directors. This control includes selection of the board and also staff of your not-for-profit serving on NFP 2's board.

☞ **HANDS ON:** Your state's arm's-length regulations are very important. Make sure you check with your funder's regulations on this issue.

Also, without this degree of separation, the IRS and/or funding agencies could legally see the two corporations as one, nullifying the value of the restructuring in some cases.

The corporations can lease space to each other and contract for management and other services at fair market values. Again, always have real leases, real contracts, signed by real people, and keep excellent records!

b. Common uses of not-for-profit subsidiaries. As noted earlier, some common uses include a foundation, a second property-holding entity, and a separation of net income. Let's examine some case studies of each.

i. *A foundation.* This is by far the most common use of a second not-for-profit. Your organization wants to establish a long-term endowment and decides that it makes sense to separate it into an additional entity.

❏ **FOR EXAMPLE:** A New England–based not-for-profit that provides residential, vocational, and recreational services to people with disabilities wanted to set aside funds for long-term investment and to have a steady income stream for its operations above and beyond its government funding. It found, in asking its donors, that many were very supportive of the idea of a foundation and saw it as a way to give to the organization the "gift that keeps on giving," that is, not just a donation that was used each year. It considered setting up a restricted fund within its existing not-for-profit corporation, but was told by these same key donors that they would be more comfortable if there was a corporate separation: They were concerned that the state funder might try to go after any endowment if it was in the primary corporation. As a result, the not-for-profit

Exhibit 10-4   A not-for-profit subsidiary.

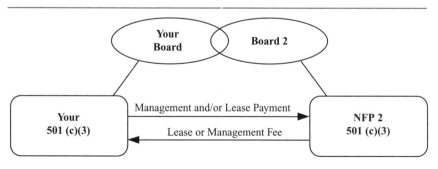

set up a second tax-exempt entity whose primary purpose was fund-raising and investment of the endowment. The not-for-profit set up a separate foundation board and asked that most of the earnings (interest and dividends) each year be given back to the not-for-profit for annual operations. As time passed, the foundation also bought (and leased at fair market value) new equipment and vehicles that the not-for-profit would have paid more for. The foundation even loaned the not-for-profit start-up funds for a new venture.

☞ **HANDS ON:** If you want to set up a second 501(c)(3) corporation and *call* it a foundation, fine, but don't have the second corporation apply for tax-exempt status *as a foundation.* If you do, you will have to comply with rigorous IRS regulations regarding annual disbursement. Be careful here, and check the IRS application before it is submitted.

☞ **HANDS ON:** If you have a restricted fund for your endowment now, and want to move it to the second not-for-profit, you can, *once the second entity receives its tax-exempt status from the IRS.* Then, you can make a donation from your not-for-profit to the second entity.

ii. *A property-holding corporation to maximize income.* In some cases, not-for-profits will have a funder who will pay for rent but not for owner-ship, even if owning a building is much cheaper in the long run. In these cases, if you have arm's length, and if you use fair market leases, you can get the best of both worlds.

❑ **FOR EXAMPLE:** An organization that helped drug abusers through res-idential treatment services needed a new building. It found a building that would be ideal, but the landlord would not invest in needed repairs. The landlord then offered to sell the building to the not-for-profit, but its main funders, the state Alcohol and Drug Agency, only funded leases, not depreciation and interest for ownership. The not-for-profit looked into its options. It established a second, arms-length organiza-tion which got a community development loan, bought and renovated the building, and leased the building to the primary not-for-profit. With the low-interest loan, the fair-market lease rate was higher than the loan payments, and cash for future renovations and equipment purchases built up in the second agency. By this careful application of a new cor-porate structure, the not-for-profit was able to meet its funders' regula-tions, but still benefit from ownership.

☞ **HANDS ON:** Make sure that the charitable purpose for your second corporation notes support of your existing not-for-profit and its charitable purposes. In this document, you would also want to include the "holding and leasing of property" in the charitable purpose.

iii. *A separation of net income to avoid grant reductions.* Some government agencies, foundations, and United Ways can be punitive in their approach to funding. In some communities, if your organization earns income from other sources, funders will reduce their support accordingly. To prevent this from happening, a second not-for-profit can be established to retain earnings. These retained earnings can be used for charitable purposes such as purchasing needed equipment for your organization.

❏ **FOR EXAMPLE:** A women's shelter in the upper Midwest received funding for domestic and sexual abuse prevention and sheltering families that were abused. The funding came from a collaboration of state, county, and foundation sources, but the collaborative funding committee had a limitation on the agency that it could not retain more than 30 days operating cash from one year to the next. (I don't have time here to tell you how dumb this is, but it does still happen.) The organization was very successful and was approached by two school systems in a nearby state to come in (for a fee) to counsel high school students on ways to avoid abuse. The counseling services were paid at a rate that would result in an annual profit above the 30-days level allowed by the organization's primary funders. In addition, the organization published three books on community sexual abuse prevention and began to sell them at conferences and over the Internet. More profits to worry about. The solution? Set up an additional arm's-length organization where the income, expenses, and profits were housed. This would not have worked if the second organization was a controlled entity—only if it was uncontrolled.

Again, most organizations that need a second corporation turn to what they know—a second not-for-profit. Its rules and regulations are familiar, and it raises the least eyebrows in the community.

3. A For-Profit Subsidiary
The next most-common type of additional corporation is a for-profit subsidiary. Here's how it works.

a. A generic for-profit model. Exhibit 10-5 shows an example of a for-profit subsidiary. Your not-for-profit can establish a for-profit corporation

Exhibit 10-5   A for-profit subsidiary.

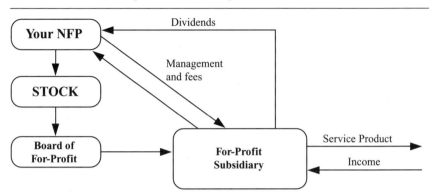

and own all the for-profit's stock. The board members of the for-profit can be from your board, but it is wise to also recruit board members with specialties related to the business that the for-profit will operate. For instance, two of the board members can be on your board, and three can be from the general community with special expertise in whatever the venture will do.

Because the not-for-profit owns all the stock, it controls who sits on the board. On an annual basis, profits from the for-profit corporation can be paid to the NFP as dividends. *Note:* The for-profit business always pays tax on its profits based on the present corporate tax rates. Your NFP and its for-profit subsidiary can contract with each other for an array of services and office space at fair market values.

b. Common uses of the for-profit model. Why would you develop a for-profit as opposed to a not-for-profit? After all, *the for-profit always pays taxes, even if the business it is in would be related to your not-for-profit's charitable purpose.* There are some valid reasons, and let's examine them.

i. *Political shelter.* If the business operated by the organization is operated within a for-profit corporation, you avoid the cries of unfair competition from the business community that often are created when a not-for-profit begins to compete with traditional businesses. As a for-profit, the business has no unfair advantage and pays taxes just like any other corporation. The irony here is that, if you have unrelated income in a not-for-profit, you pay taxes as well, but once the slings and arrows are out, no one ever wants to hear that. So, if the political price is really high, you might fold your venture into a for-profit and declare that you are on a level playing field with your competition.

ii. *Less expensive capital.* For-profit entities can often obtain capital easier than not-for-profits, and most government loan and loan guarantee programs are only available to for-profits. In addition, banks and other lenders understand for-profits far better than they understand NFPs. We discussed this at length in Chapter 9, Financing Your Entrepreneurship. Thus, you may find that the access to capital or the interest rate benefits outweigh the cost of taxation. Be careful here to really run the numbers in the best case, worst case, and middle ground. Again, let me emphasize: Once you establish the for-profit, you are locked into taxes on profits forever, *no matter what the business does.*

❑ **FOR EXAMPLE:** A not-for-profit that employed people with disabilities in regular community employment had a janitorial service. It cleaned various offices each evening, training its clients to do the work needed. The business made money, but since the mission statement of the organization included the language "train for competitive employment and provide integrated work environments for long-term employment," the income was related and untaxable. The organization planned a major expansion, developed its business plan, and needed $200,000 in financing. As it looked at its options, it found that a low-interest loan package offered through the mayor's office was the best bet, saving nearly 4 percent on interest per year. But that funding was only targeted at for-profits: The not-for-profit didn't qualify. The organization set up a for-profit subsidiary to run the business, which was capitalized by a loan from the not-for-profit as well as the $200,000 from the city.

The result? The 4 percent saved on the loan over the term of the loan (10 years) results in $46,782 in interest savings, a significant amount. But, as the organization was projecting just over $347,000 in profits in the same 10-year period, the federal taxes alone were over $53,500. And then there were state taxes. So, the organization spent more than it saved, even though the service was identical in the for-profit or in the not-for-profit corporate configuration.

iii. *Take on a partner.* A for-profit environment allows you to take on a partner, someone or some organization that has money or expertise that you need. While this is an option, I have some advice for you, and I want to be clear about this, so here goes:

DON'T DO IT!

Selling part of your business to someone else is a bad thing about 99.999 percent of the time. The only reason I even mention it is that people continue to think it is such a cool idea, such an easy way to raise cheap money. "Oh, I know," they say, "We'll just sell some stock and get our money that way. I know we have some donors that would be pleased with our businesslike approach." True, they may be, and they may be the nicest people in the world, but even if their motives are not suspect, I always caution you with the words of my father. Dad was a corporate secretary of a Fortune 500 company, the poor guy who had to deal with stockholders, their families, their accountants, their attorneys, and, *when they died, the executors of their estates.* His words of wisdom, borne of painful experience were these: "The day after you sell stock to your best friend or the nicest person in the world, someone who would never give you any trouble at all, that wonderful soul will die and have the biggest S.O.B. in the world as his or her executor, someone whose job it is to maximize the value of the estate—in other words, to take you for all you are worth."

Cheap capital? Free money? Ha! *Don't do it.*

c. Things to remember. As the for-profit format is a bit different, I need to emphasize some other issues for you to remember:

- Dividends from a controlled subsidiary (if your organization owns 80 percent or more of the subsidiary, which I hope you will) are *not* considered taxable income to the not-for-profit parent. They have already been taxed within the for-profit as profits.

- If the not-for-profit owns 80 percent or more of the subsidiary, and the subsidiary pays interest income (or certain royalties) to the parent not-for-profit, the parent will pay unrelated business income taxes on the interest income to the IRS, based on current corporate rates.

- A transfer of funds from a controlled for-profit subsidiary to a parent not-for-profit will be treated as a dividend. A dividend is not a deductible expense for the for-profit. The for-profit must pay tax on its profits *before* paying dividends to its parent corporation. Thus, you can't just donate all your profits away. Nice try, but the IRS is ahead of you and will always take its part.

- Management fees to your not-for-profit, earned either from a for-profit or a not-for-profit subsidiary, may or may not be considered unrelated income. If it is unrelated, and your fees are higher than your associated expenses, you'll have a tax bill. *Note:* At the time of this writing, legislation had been introduced in Congress making such income related. Check with the IRS.

- A for-profit subsidiary cannot be considered an arm's-length entity as long as you own more than 50 percent of the stock. Thus, you cannot comply with arm's-length requirements of most funders. Remember this as you consider setting up this form of second entity.

4. An Umbrella Corporation

Umbrella corporations are entities that are superior (controlling) to more than one related or unrelated subsidiary. They are usually set up to allow a traditional board of directors to oversee the activities of more than one other corporation or partnership and are often set up by a service corporation superior to it.

The way that the umbrella controls its subsidiaries varies greatly. The entities may be controlled or uncontrolled. The umbrella may provide all or some of the management and accounting. The boards may interlock or be identical. The subsidiaries may be distinguished for reasons of potential liability, differing missions or accounting, or economies of scale.

Umbrella setups require a great deal of record keeping, tax work, and accounting to keep everything straight. They are unnecessary more often than they are valuable but, in the right setting and with careful planning, the right staff and board of directors, this type of corporation can be the perfect tool for a successful business venture. A sample corporate structuring is shown on the left in Exhibit 10-6.

5. A Cooperative

Cooperatives are unusual entities, ones whose control is the most critical element. They can be (and are) large or small, for-profit or not-for-profit. Some co-ops are huge, such as Ocean Spray or Sunkist, some are small, such as grain elevators.

Exhibit 10-6   A holding corporation.

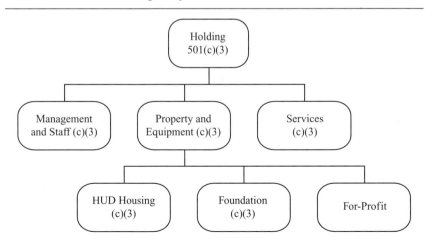

a. A generic cooperative model. For you, the applications of this model would probably come if you wanted a structure that allowed you to cooperate (hence the name) with other not-for-profits on a joint venture. (See Exhibit 10-7.)

Co-ops are very egalitarian. They require equal control of the board no matter what the size of the individual member's stake or ownership. Thus, the largest member has the same vote as the smallest. This is much different than in a standard corporation, where a 51 percent owner can do pretty much whatever he or she wants, despite being numerically outnumbered by 10 other stockholders who jointly own the remaining 49 percent.

Just as with a corporation, however, any profits are distributed by size or by percentage of investment.

This structure really appeals to most not-for-profits because the big organizations can't run roughshod over the small ones.

b. Some uses of cooperatives. How would you use a co-op? Here are some examples.

i. *Joint venture.* You need to work with other not-for-profits to apply for certain long-term funding. You can't come to an agreement about which organization will be the primary contractor, so you establish a cooperative

Exhibit 10-7   A cooperative.

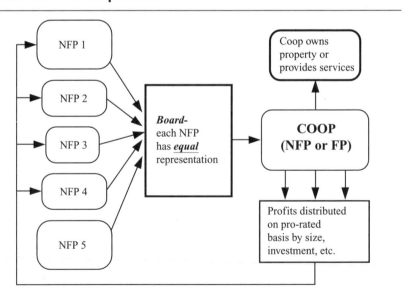

to run the contract, with each participant becoming a partner and having representation on the board.

ii. *Credit unions.* Credit union? Yep, and before you move onto the next section, stop and think: You can't pay your staff what they are worth, and neither can your not-for-profit peers in the community. What about setting up a credit union for all not-for-profit employees, and offer savings, loans, and so forth. There are lots of rules and regulations to abide by, but it is being done around the country by communities of not-for-profits, and the model they use is the cooperative.

iii. *Property.* Perhaps you have the opportunity to acquire a large building, but can't fill all of it. You approach other not-for-profits, but they don't want to lease any longer, either, so they won't become your tenants. But they will become your partners, and then you use the cooperative model. Through the co-op, you all own the building and equally vote on items such as repairs, refinancing, or remodeling. Again, there is a lot of precedent for this use of co-ops.

So, there are the most common types of not-for-profit corporate structures. Before we go, let's repeat the mantra of corporate structuring one more time:

a. Keep it simple.

b. Document everything.

c. Keep time sheets for anyone who is working for more than one corporation.

And remember, the cost of the corporation (including record keeping, taxation, and the audit) *must be less than the benefits the corporation produces.*

These marvelous tools have limited uses. If you decide to pursue using one of the tools, get some help, and get it early. Consult your corporate attorney, your accountant, your key funders, and perhaps, a consultant who has done this kind of work for a not-for-profit before.

RECAP

This was a technical, but important, chapter. You gained a lot of information that could, in certain situations, make or break your entrepreneurial endeavors. First, we looked at the Unrelated Business Income Tax (UBIT). I told you that the key issue was the wording of your mission statement and showed you the IRS tests on the subject which were as follows:

1. Is this business venture a trade or business?

2. Is the business regularly carried out with the frequency of a like commercial venture?

3. Is it unrelated to our tax-exempt organization's mission and purpose?

   a. Does it significantly contribute to our organization's mission?

   b. Is the scope of our business venture appropriate? Is the business operating this business outside the geographic boundaries stated in the bylaws? Is the size of the business activity appropriate?

   c. Is the beneficiary class appropriate?

I also cautioned you that the tax is liable only on profits, not on income, even though it is called the Unrelated Business *Income* Tax! Remember, unrelated income should always have some level of unrelated expenses along with it. I also provided you with a decision flow chart that should help you work through the issue.

Then, we turned to your options in corporate structuring. I told you three important rules about corporate structures which were as follows:

a. Keep it simple.

b. Document everything.

c. Keep time sheets for anyone who is working for more than one corporation.

We went over the major benefits, drawbacks, and uses of four corporate models. These were as follows:

A second not-for-profit

A for-profit subsidiary

An umbrella corporation

A cooperative

I also strongly cautioned you about taking on for-profit partners. These tools are now in place for you to use should the situation arise. Some readers will use this information immediately. Others may never need it. But at least it is here for you to refer back to when and if you do need it.

There are a couple of other issues to cover before your social entrepreneurial training is complete. The last two chapters will cover these. We'll start with how and why your funders should encourage your entrepreneurial activities and finish with ways that you can keep your entrepreneurial actions focused on mission outcomes.

QUESTIONS FOR DISCUSSION: CHAPTER 10

1. Are we liable for UBIT now? Do we file a 990T every year?

2. What if our venture is subject to UBIT? Are there ways we can amend the venture or our mission statement to avoid it?

3. Are there any applications of corporate structures that make sense now? How about within the time line of our strategic plan?

11

Social Entrepreneurism for Funders

OVERVIEW

In this chapter you will learn about the following:

➤ Why Funders Should Embrace Entrepreneurism
➤ What Funders Can Do to Encourage Entrepreneurism

By this point, you have not only learned a great deal about social entrepreneurism, you have covered all the key steps in moving your organization down the road to becoming an organization that exhibits the necessary characteristics of an entrepreneur: risk taking, flexibility, a focus on mission and markets, and a passion for constant innovation and improvement. Lots of things can get in your way, or can distract you from your journey. You can be less than totally successful at convincing your staff or board that entrepreneurism is a good thing for your organization and the people you serve. You can lose focus, as a result of a fiscal, personnel, or management crisis, and go back to your old ways.

Or you can run into trouble with your primary funder or funders. Since they hold the purse strings, the policies and opinions of your key funding streams do matter, and if those policies intentionally or inadvertently prevent you from becoming entrepreneurial, you have much less maneuvering room and may even have to postpone implementing your entrepreneurial strategy.

So you need your funders on board, and this chapter is provided to help you convince them that they should join you on the entrepreneurial journey: Your becoming an entrepreneurial organization benefits the funder just as much as it does your organization and the people you serve. In the following pages, I will show you why funders, be they a unit of government, a foundation, a corporate donor, or a United Way, should do everything in their power to facilitate, encourage, and enable you to become and remain a social entrepreneur. Then, I'll specifically list the things that funders should and shouldn't do to foster the entrepreneurial outcomes that they (and you) want. I hope that, after you read these pages, you will show them to your key funders, perhaps meeting with them afterward to discuss ways that you can work together to provide better services, sooner, and to more people for the available resources. Because that, at its core, is the point of social entrepreneurism, isn't it?

Note: The remainder of this chapter will be written specifically for your funders. I will speak to them directly, which will make it easier for them when you give them copies of this chapter.

A. WHY FUNDERS SHOULD EMBRACE ENTREPRENEURISM

If you are reading these pages and you represent an organization that provides funding to or purchases services from not-for-profit organizations, you probably have been given this text by a staff member or volunteer of one of those organizations. This material is from a book written for not-for-profits who want to become better providers of their services and who are pursuing this organizational improvement through a concept called social entrepreneurism. This chapter is written specifically for those organizations that provide funding to not-for-profits to encourage you to consider the concept and to be aware of what your organization can do to enable the not-for-profits you interact with to become and remain more mission-capable.

1. What Is Social Entrepreneurism?

Social entrepreneurism is not a new idea, but to some it sounds like an oxymoron. How can organizations that are focused on social good be concerned with becoming entrepreneurs? Don't the two conflict, and doesn't becoming an entrepreneur distract the not-for-profit staff and board from pursuing their mission?

Just the opposite. The very core of social entrepreneurism is good stewardship and better pursuit of mission. Good stewards don't just rest on their laurels, they try new things, serve people in new ways, are lifelong learners, and try to have their organizations be centers of excellence. Social entrepreneurs have these characteristics:

- They are willing to take reasonable risk on behalf of the people that their organization serves.
- They are constantly looking for new ways to serve their constituencies and to add value to existing services.

- They understand that all resource allocations are really stewardship investments.
- They weigh the social and financial return of each of these investments.
- They understand the difference between needs and wants.
- They always keep mission first, but know that without money, there is no mission output.

For a funding agency like yours, it seems to me that mission is also the bottom line, but that you need to help the not-for-profits for which you provide funds to adapt to the new, more competitive, and more accountable environment that they find themselves in. In many cases, traditional forms of funding and oversight do just the opposite, and I know that you don't want to stand in the way of organizations becoming better mission producers. I also recognize that change of this magnitude takes time for all parties to adjust to: the not-for-profits, their communities, and the people and organizations that provide funding to them.

You may represent a corporation, an arm of government, a foundation, a United Way, or some other funding source. As a result of my trying to address a wide range of funders, the observations in the following pages are broad, and not all will concern you or your methods of purchasing services. But some of my suggestions will certainly hit home, and I hope that they provide you with some food for thought on ways that you can be a better mission enabler, because more mission outcomes are what all of us want.

2. How Does Social Entrepreneurism Help Make Not-for-Profits Better?

If you are concerned about developing and working with outcome-oriented, totally focused, more independent, self-reliant not-for-profits, then social entrepreneurism is for you. These are but a few of the ways that this line of thinking makes the organization you fund better. Here are some other specific ways that social entrepreneurs make for better not-for-profits.

- *Social entrepreneurism results in the provision of more direct mission of higher quality.* Why? Because the vast majority (95 percent) of the organizations that I have helped develop business plans for new businesses have developed businesses that provided direct services. This makes sense from two perspectives: the not-for-profit knows that business, and by expanding in that area, it supports its mission. Additionally, by focusing more on what they do well rather than just chasing dollars, social entrepreneurs ramp up their quality levels throughout the refocused agency.

- *More money for more mission.* Social entrepreneurs find more dollars by expanding the number of people they serve, the areas they
serve, and the way that they serve. Where they used to see plain old
expenditures, they now see investments in the community. What they
used to think of as public information, they now know as marketing.
Where they used to be focused only on meeting needs, they now
match needs with wants. All of this results in happier people—the
people they serve, the people (like you) who often pay for the service, the people they employ, and the people that volunteer for them.
And, social entrepreneurs are tireless seekers of new markets, new
ways to serve. All of this results in more money—often not from your
organization—which can be used for more mission.

- *Social entrepreneurism makes your job easier.* First, social entrepreneurs will start to look at you and your organization as a valued
customer rather than someone to "get money from." Sadly, I know
hundreds of not-for-profit managers who think of their biggest funder as their worst enemy, someone to joust with and complain about
rather than someone to provide customer service to. So, over time,
the organizations who think like social entrepreneurs will begin to
change their attitude about their funders: you.

  Second, social entrepreneurs are focused on outcomes, not on
process. For most funders reading this, outcome measures are
increasingly important and meeting major resistance from too many
organizations. You will catch much less grief from your social entrepreneur contractors than from your not-for-profit agencies that still
think of themselves as charities.

  Third, most funders want to buy services from innovative and
quality-driven organizations. Social entrepreneurs are both. Their
outcomes must be all high quality, and they are constant innovators.
Both of these facts make your interactions with them more rewarding
and your decisions to contract with them easier to justify.

  Finally, social entrepreneurs look at your organization as one
group that purchases services from them, but not as the only lifeboat
on the ocean. Admittedly, this can be hard for some funding agencies
who have thought of themselves as the patron of the organization, but
in both the short and long term, this increasing sense of self-
sufficiency will build stronger community service organizations, and
thus stronger communities. Your agency's long-term goal is, I am
sure, to improve the communities where you provide money, so this
outcome means that you can get more mission for your money, help
in a particular way, and then spread your funds and your interest to

other communities sooner. Not a bad bargain for giving up some control and oversight.

3. Why Should Your Organization Support Not-for-Profit Entrepreneurism?

In summary, let me collect all the rationales from the preceding pages in one place to state my case. Supporting social entrepreneurism

- Results in more mission, of more quality, to more people
- Results in stronger, more independent, and innovative community service organizations
- Puts the relationship between community service organizations and the organizations that purchase services from them, like yours, on a more reasonable, more accountable, and more professional basis
- Uses your organization's funds more wisely, with more mission outcome per dollar

I know, from thousands of conversations with funding agency staff, that these are things that you want. So, if I have (and I sincerely hope that I have) convinced you, how can you help? How can you encourage and facilitate more entrepreneurial activities and attitudes at the community service organizations that you interact with? That's the subject of the next section.

B. WHAT FUNDERS CAN DO TO ENCOURAGE ENTREPRENEURISM

In this section, I want to propose some things that you as a funder can do to encourage the spread of social entrepreneurism. I hope by this point that I have convinced you that social entrepreneurism is both a good idea and one that benefits the community. In the following pages, I'll outline 11 ideas that can turbocharge SE's development in the not-for-profits you work with. Some relate to the way that you fund, while others are attitude changes both internally as well as the way that you interact with other organizations. I'm sure that some of my comments and ideas will concern and, perhaps, even upset you. I will challenge some long held beliefs and some well-entrenched schools of thought. All I ask is that you hear me out completely before you decide what you will or will not do regarding social entrepreneurship.

Before we get to specific ways that you can help, I have to make a few overall observations. The first is that most, but not all, funders need an attitude adjustment in terms of the way that they see their relationship with community service organizations. Instead of thinking of not-for-profits as charities, you need to start thinking of them as mission-based businesses, ones from whom you purchase services. Think of the not-for-profits that you fund as vendors, not subsidiaries. You purchase services, you don't provide subsidies. For far too long, we've treated our not-for-profits as poor stepchildren and, as a result, have held them back from achieving their potential.

Here are my three core philosophies about not-for-profits and how they relate to your organization.

- *Not-for-profits are really mission-based businesses.* The idea that not-for-profits are businesses, in the business of providing the best possible mission outcomes to the community, is not one that sits well in some sectors. Some people prefer to think of these organizations as charities, poorer, less well organized and managed than a traditional for-profit business. While this may have been acceptable in the past, why should we agree with it today? Why shouldn't we want our community service organizations to be well run, well organized, well marketed, and financially sound? Of course we should, and this philosophy of thinking of 501(c)(3)s as businesses in the business of doing mission goes a long way toward making that a reality. If you continue to look at the not-for-profit community as second-class citizens, they can never achieve their full potential.

- *Not-for-profits earn every dime of their income.* Again we're going up against traditional perspectives that not-for-profits are funded, they are subsidized, they are "given funds." In reality, not-for-profits earn every dime they take in as income, including their charitable donations. Look at it this way: When you send a community service organization some funding, do you just send them a check? Of course not. You want something for it, normally a certain kind of service provided in a certain way to a certain segment of the community. That is called purchasing services. It is exactly the same as your contracting with me to do a day of training. You are buying a service. That is the totality of the transaction, nothing more, nothing less. Even people who donate money are really purchasing services for someone they probably will never meet.

  This idea means that not-for-profits earn *all* their money—thus, *they don't get subsidies.* Subsidies are things that people get for doing nothing. Getting paid for not growing a field of wheat, now *that's* a subsidy. Getting food stamps is a subsidy. Providing a service for a certain amount of money, that's earned income. Community service organizations earn their money, since they do something for it.

- *Not-for-profits can and should make money.* I know, I know, this is a real problem for many funding organizations. First, the legality. There is no state or federal law, no state or federal regulation that says that not-for-profit 501(c)(3)s cannot earn a profit. It flat out does not exist. In fact, Congress not only acknowledges that not-for-profits can make money, the House and the Senate *want* these organizations to keep their profits and reinvest them in the community! How do I know this? Because when a not-for-profit gets its 501(c)(3) tax status, it gets an exemption from paying taxes on net income (profits) earned from activities that are related to its mission statement. Congress wanted to encourage charitable activities, so they gave the (c)(3)s an exemption from taxes on their profits. Think about it, now. If the (c)(3)s couldn't make a profit, they wouldn't need a tax exemption, would they?

  In fact, much of traditional funding policy flies right in the face of Congress's intent—it takes back the profits, or undercuts them. We'll deal with ways to fix funding in my specific ideas on how to encourage social entrepreneurism in a little bit. But let me say here that part of the problem is the way we refer to 501 (c)(3)s. We call then *non-profits* or *not-for-profits,* which both refer to what they are *not* and gives the false impression that they should *not* make money. I would much rather we renamed the sector *community service organizations,* which is what these entities *are.*

  In any event, 501 (c)(3)s both can make money, and they should. Why? Because by making money they can innovate, grow, try new ways of providing service, meet community needs faster and in a more locally sensitive manner. Without profits they remain what many, far too many, are today: financially indentured servants of funders like you. Indentured servitude went by the wayside in the nineteenth century in this country, except for our community service organizations. It is now the twenty-first century. Don't you think that it is time to emancipate our 501(c)(3)s? I do.

Let's review these three important shifts in thought. They are as follows:

- Not-for-profits are really mission-based businesses.
- Not-for-profits earn every dime of their income.
- Not-for-profits can and should make money.

Enough of the theory. Below are 11 specific things you and your organization can do to encourage social entrepreneurism. Read them all through and then consider which apply to you and your organization. Most will, with the exception of, perhaps, some of the funding change ideas. For example, your funding policies may not include a requirement for match, or may not require or encourage an end-of-year spend down. However, most of these will apply to you. What can you do soon, today, this week, this fiscal year to start the entrepreneurial ball rolling?

1. Encourage Innovation

This is the risk part. Your risk, and the organization's risk. But it is also the mission improvement part. Only by trying new things, or old things in new ways, can we improve the way that we provide services to our communities. Social entrepreneurs are constantly asking their customers what they want and trying to give it to them; thus, they are constantly innovating and trying new things.

When a not-for-profit that you work with comes to you and says that it is trying things a different way, encourage it. Of course, it should be able to explain why it is innovating, on what basis, and for what outcome, but the fact of innovation is good. If you have funds that can be used for innovative purposes, try to prioritize this use. One of the sad parts about the not-for-profit sector is that few if any small community service providers ever have any funds for what the for-profit world calls research and development, or R&D. And, I suspect that if they did, they wouldn't fund R&D anyway—they'd spend the money on mission right away. But you can encourage R&D, allow expenditures for it, and praise it when you see it.

2. Understand That Not All Ideas Work Out—Even Yours

This suggestion is closely linked to number 1. If your organization wants to encourage innovation and experimentation in your not-for-profit contractors, you have to acknowledge that not all ideas work out. And, when they don't pan out exactly as planned, you shouldn't pan the organization. As a society, we are much too focused on assigning blame and trumpeting failure rather than praising initiative and innovation. I hope that you had a biology, chemistry, or physics teacher in high school who told you that there are no failed experiments. Experiments begin with a hypothesis, which is then tested. If the hypothesis is proven correct, and something new is learned, the experiment is a success. If the hypothesis is proven invalid, and something new is learned, *the experiment is also a success.*

This also holds true for programs, policies, or ideas that your organization trumpets. Not every idea, every innovation, every philosophy works every time. For example, while I firmly believe in the benefits of social entrepreneurism, I know that it won't work in all organizations or communities; some have too many cultural, historical, or political barriers in place. The fact that social entrepreneurship doesn't work everywhere every time in every agency does not invalidate the idea, nor does it mean that the organization has failed or is in some way less concerned with mission.

So don't get into the blame game. As long as the organization is trying new things and learns from its experience (note the same root in *experience* and *experiment!*), it's a good thing, and one you want to encourage.

3. Provide Funding for Entrepreneurial Activities

What would some entrepreneurial activities be? Development of a marketing plan, regular asking of customers what they want, staff training (see the next section), innovation in current services, new business development, identification of core competencies, benchmarking, developing new pricing strategies, and learning more about competition. If you see these activities going on, encourage them. And, if you cannot get away from a grant mentality, at least allow these activities as a reimbursable expense.

4. Encourage Lifelong Learning

The best, most innovative, highest-quality organizations in the world constantly educate and train their staff. Unfortunately, in the not-for-profit sector, training is usually only allowed by funder for mandated tasks that are required for licensing or accreditation. Don't stop there. Encourage, even require constant learning in the organizations you contract with. Some examples would be training on marketing, customer service, market assessment, quality improvement, outcome measurement, delegation, communications, and regular board training. We live in an information age, and those with the information will be the ones we want to have providing our services. Would you really want a 55-year-old physician doing surgery on you if he or she had not kept up with the changes in medicine since the end of his or her residency? Neither would I, and I'm happy to pay for his or her continuing education. Let's do the same for people who run soup kitchens, children's museums, community theater, and who train foster parents.

5. Go to Contract for Services

This is the first of my six admonitions about funding policy, and it is the most important. As noted earlier, you are a purchaser of services, not a funder of programs. That is, you buy things (usually services) from community service organizations. This is consistent with my philosophy that not-for-profits earn all their money. If this is true, you need to go to a system in which you buy outcomes, not fund entities. You buy things from the companies that sell you computers, or phone service, or clean your offices. They just happen to be for-profit businesses. Why should it be any different with a mission-based business? It shouldn't.

Move, if you haven't already, to a purchase-of-service form of funding. For $X, you buy Y number of mission units. I understand that this is not always as easy as it sounds, but most organizations can develop a unit cost for what they do—if you force them to. Work with your community service organizations to develop purchasable units of service that you can buy and that you can evaluate.

6. Bid Stuff

The second part of the funding change needs to be more competition. The best way to get more mission for the money is to bid out your purchases of service. Competition forces improvements in quality and reductions (or at least containment) of costs quicker than any other force in nature. Now, I am well aware that in some communities there is only one choice of organizations to provide a particular service, but that is because we've lived for 50 years with the mantra that competition (aka duplication of service) is a *bad* thing in the social services when it is a *good* thing everywhere else. Competition is good if your long-term objective is more service, better service, and less-expensive service. Now, I am not suggesting that we should leave the entire social service, arts, environmental, and educational arenas to the for-profit community. We need people and organizations who are social entrepreneurs and focused on mission first, but that doesn't mean that they aren't smart, flexible, or capable enough to compete. Again, competition is good for mission outcomes, not bad. Bid your purchases of service.

7. Don't Punish Efficiency or Good Management

Many, many funders are prone to do this in the guise of "use it or lose it" funding. And again this only seems to hold for not-for-profits. Why should an organization that has done what it promised to do in terms of service provision have to give back what it didn't spend? If I work for your organization providing training, and we agree on a price and a scope of work, you won't come to me asking for "excess revenue," because there is no such thing. Do you ask for excess revenue at McDonald's or from Federal Express? Of course not. You pay the price, and if you don't get what you pay for, you go somewhere else.

Rewarding efficiency is a good thing, not a bad one. If you get what you paid for from a community service provider, and it does the work at the level of quality that you require, why shouldn't it keep any leftover funds? The money is now that provider's. It's no longer yours. *The service provider earned it.*

A second way that funders often punish community service providers is by not letting them have adequate (or even any) financial reserves. To start with, what business is it of yours? If you purchase services from me, do you really care if I am rich or poor? What you care about is whether I did a good job, fulfilled my contract, and charged you what we agreed on. Why is there this obsession with not-for-profits having to be poor to be holy? It particularly pervades state governments and United Ways, with certain foundations coming in a close second.

Even more odd, this perception seems to be true only for small to medium-sized not-for-profits. It's okay for a hospital, college, or private school to have an endowment or a reasonable cash reserve, but not for the local soup kitchen. Hmmm. Why?

Stop doing this, if you are an agency that practices this damaging form of funding. If you do make the change, you also get a hidden benefit. If an agency bids on some service, and gets the contract, it must then provide the service for the agreed-upon price. If it overspends *that's its problem*, not yours. Don't let the agency come whining to you to bail it out. Remember, you are buying services, not acting as a foster parent for charities.

8. Fund Overhead

I understand that organizations that only fund "direct costs" are intent on getting the most for their money. But they must not have taken Budgeting 101. All organizations have some fixed expenses, some administrative overhead, and they have to be paid for. You're saying that you artificially won't pay for them just makes the organizations do something equally artificial: cost shifting. Once they start cost shifting, they begin what I call the downward spiral of self-delusion. Direct cost funding along with matching funding (see the next item on my list) lead to not-for-profits having done so much financial adjusting that they have no real idea of what things really cost. In a competitive era, this leads to real trouble.

Look at it another way. Just paying for direct costs is like the two of us going to a professional baseball game, and you going up to the ticket seller and telling it, "I want two tickets, but there is no way I'm paying $50. Just give me a ticket that includes my share of the costs of the salaries of the guys who will play tonight." Would you be embarrassed asking for that kind of deal? So would I. So, why aren't you embarrassed when you ask for that from a not-for-profit?

9. End Match

I also am well aware of the theory of matching funds. It shows community support, collaboration, and so on and so on. It also reduces your costs, which is not a bad thing. But not only does it encourage cost shifting and all of its concomitant ills, it also says one thing loud and clear to the not-for-profits you buy from: "What you are providing is of so *little* value to me that I am not willing to pay full price." And, as a result, we have nearly a million not-for-profits that are unprepared to compete, because they think that competition is always about price. It's not, it's always about *value*. Do you value what your not-for-profit service providers do? Then pay for it. How do you keep your costs under control? You bid the contract and encourage competition and innovation.

10. Don't Worry about What's Not in the Contract

Too many funders, starting with the federal government, seem to think that, once you take any money from them, they own you. Sounds like indentured servitude to me. And this leads to all kinds of ridiculous, expensive, non-mission-producing oversight. Remember, you are a purchaser of service, not the IRS, nor the attorney general. Why should you care if the not-for-profit has another not-for-profit as a subsidiary? Why should you care if it owns or leases its building, or whether it has an endowment? What you should care about is whether it did the job, provided the service you contracted with it to provide, on time, with high quality, and for the cost agreed upon.

Leave the legal stuff to the enforcement agencies, such as the IRS, who have many, many rules covering the operation and financing of not-for-profits; or your attorney general, who has a similar quiver full of rules and regulations, and any accrediting bodies that inspect the agencies you contract with. Stick to the contract, stick to business, and let the other stuff go. You'll save money, save time, save headaches, and so will the agencies you contract with.

11. Encourage Competition, Not Just Collaboration

The past few years have seen a marked increase in not-for-profit mergers, as agencies struggle to keep costs down by getting bigger and taking advantage of what the business world calls economies of scale. At the same time, I see foundations and state funders calling for collaboration, and even forcing it sometimes. There is a place for collaboration, and I certainly support it when it occurs naturally. But to force fit it is like trying to arrange a marriage: There usually isn't a good match.

If it is important to you to encourage collaboration, fine. But do it as a stop-gap measure on the way to a more competitive, more mission-capable community. Because that is where you want your not-for-profits to be. And when they get there, you'll be purchasing services from well-managed, flexible, high-quality, market-driven, mission-based organizations. Then everyone wins, particularly the end user of the services you purchase.

Now that you have read my suggestions, I pose the question again. What can you do soon to start encouraging entrepreneurism? I know that many of my ideas will require systemic changes in policy, perhaps even in statute or regulation for government funders. But just because it is a long journey does not mean you shouldn't take the first step.

Social entrepreneurs will be the best, highest-quality, most successful, and most mission-driven community service providers of the twenty-first century. As an organization that purchases services, you are in a crucial position that can either help or impede their success. The choice is yours, and it is not an insignificant one. I hope you are willing to share some of the risk that social entrepreneurs are ready to take on behalf of the people in the community and make the right choice.

RECAP

In this chapter we've covered social entrepreneurism from the perspective of the organizations who most often pay for the services that social entrepreneurs provide: government agencies, foundations, corporations, and United Ways. I wrote directly for the funders, in the hope that people who purchase this book would share this chapter with their primary funder or funders.

First, we talked about what social entrepreneurism is and how it benefits the community, the community service organization, and the organizations that fund them. I showed how SE organizations provide more service at a higher level of quality sooner.

Next, I made some observations as to why a funding entity should support social entrepreneurism. We noted that supporting SE

- Results in more mission, of more quality, to more people.
- Results in stronger, more independent, and innovative community service organizations.
- Puts the relationship between community service organizations and the organizations that purchase services from them on a more reasonable, more accountable, and more professional basis.
- Uses an organization's funds more wisely, with more mission outcome per dollar.

I then turned to the issue of how to help, but started with a review of needed changes in the relationship between funding agencies and community service organizations. I reviewed my three core philosophies about not-for-profits which are the following:

Not-for-profits are really mission-based businesses.

Not-for-profits earn every dime of their income.

Not-for-profits can and should make money.

Finally, I listed my 11 suggestions for ways that funding organizations can encourage social entrepreneurism. These were as follows:

1. Encourage innovation.
2. Understand that not all ideas work out.
3. Provide funding for entrepreneurial activities.
4. Encourage lifelong learning.
5. Go to contract for services.
6. Bid stuff.
7. Don't punish efficiency.
8. Fund overhead.
9. End match.
10. Don't worry about what's not in the contract.
11. Encourage competition not just collaboration.

One final note to funders: These ideas will start the discussion inside your funding organization. I also hope that you will look at the rest of this book as a resource for other not-for-profits that are considering starting down the social entrepreneurial path.

QUESTIONS FOR DISCUSSION: CHAPTER 11

1. Are there funders of ours that will embrace entrepreneurism? Are there those that won't?

2. How can we work with our key funders to convince them that social entrepreneurship is a good thing for everyone?

3. Would it help us to change the way that we communicate with our funders about our activities? Should we try to set goals with them that support both our entrepreneurial activities and their organizational priorities?

4. Should we share this chapter with our funders? Which ones? With what kind of introduction?

12

Final Thoughts

OVERVIEW

In this chapter you will learn about the following:

- ➤ Holding on to Your Core Values
- ➤ Making Sure That Mission, Not Just Money, Is the Bottom Line
- ➤ Final Thoughts

You know an awful lot about what it takes to become and maintain a culture of social entrepreneurism in your mission-based organization. You've learned about business development models, how to instill the entrepreneurial spirit in your board and staff, how to use technical tools, find financing, and how to write feasibility studies and business plans. I hope that you have started implementing some of this, and begun to journey to a state of constant entrepreneurial vigilance, innovation, and adaptation to the ever changing wants of your markets and your community.

But there is a dark side to the social entrepreneur's journey. Is it possible for that change to build up too much momentum and to go from being a positive change to a juggernaut out of control? Yes. And in this final chapter, I want to arm you with some cautions and cautionary tales to help you avoid negative outcomes, ones that could reduce your mission capabilities rather than enhance them.

First, we'll examine how to hold on to your core organizational values as you, your staff, and board become social entrepreneurs. Then, I'll give you some guidance in how to make sure that mission, and not just money, is always your ultimate bottom line. You've gotten yourself up and into the entrepreneurial saddle. Let's make sure you can make the beast go in the direction that most helps your organization, your mission, and the people you serve.

Last but not least, I'll give you some final thoughts to, hopefully, spur you on to even greater mission achievements.

A. HOLDING ON TO YOUR CORE VALUES

To paraphrase the old commercial: It's 11 P.M. Do you know where your values are tonight? Seriously, do you have a written statement of organizational values that accompanies your mission? If you don't, you should have. Why? Because there are times when you are going to need the guidance that those values provide to keep you on the straight and narrow path of mission delivery.

You see, entrepreneurism is great. It allows you to try new things, meet new needs, and serve more people, more efficiently, sooner. That's the good news. The dark side of the Force is that entrepreneurism is also very, very seductive. It is exciting, alluring, and for many, something new and fascinating. And, with all this appeal, it can take you down roads you don't want to travel. You can wake up one day and find out that, in the avid pursuit of becoming a social entrepreneur, you lost your mission focus and are just another business.

This book has been full of techniques, methods, suggestions, checklists, and advice on how to move your organization onto a more entrepreneurial footing; how to take good risks on behalf of good people, for a good reason. And that good reason is your mission. If, at the end, you use the techniques to distract yourself from your mission, then I have done you harm rather than good. So, let's begin by looking at some problems that can crop up on the entrepreneurial journey and how you can avoid or overcome them.

1. Markets That Move Outside of Your Values Envelope

With the fast pace of change today you have to understand that at some time, some market, whether it is a purchaser of service, a collaborator, or a service recipient, will ask you to do something that is outside your values envelope. Unlike test pilots, who are paid to push the very outside edges of their aircraft's performance envelope, you are not employed to see how close you can bring your organization to the precipice of abandoning your values. In both cases, there can be a disastrous crash. The difference? The pilot wears a parachute to work. You don't.

❏ **FOR EXAMPLE:** There flat out is no better example of this than managed care. This system of reimbursement and oversight is designed based on an excellent premise: that we should pay our health care providers to keep us healthy rather than reward them when we are sick. The risk-reward mechanism was set up to pay health care providers a flat rate per person per year, whether that person was sick or not. In its early stages, managed care really did help, by reducing unnecessary tests, lowering average hospital stays, and making care a bit more rational. Then, as too often happens, the pendulum swung too far. We all heard stories of new mothers being kicked out of the hospital 24 hours after delivering, or of cancer patients being denied needed pain medication. These decisions were nearly always made by a non–health care professional, and therein lies the moral of the tale. Health care providers have a singular set of values. Accountants and business executives have another set. Not better, not worse, just different. At first the medical practitioners went along. But over time the doctors and nurses got pushed way too far out of their values envelope, and now you see physicians breaking their ties to managed care organizations, and even discussing unionization. It is a response to a values violation more than anything else.

☞ **HANDS ON:** You need a check and balance in this area. Whenever you are asked to do something new, or provide a different service, or the same service in a different way, or consider moving into providing services for a new population or community, run the idea by a randomly selected group of staff and board. Ask them this: "Are we okay doing this based on our mission and values? Why? Why not? Are you comfortable with this change?" *Really listen* to their answers. And, note that my suggestion is that you use a *different* set of people *each* time rather than just assigning this issue to a permanent values committee. Why? Because by doing this, you spread around the input, get more people involved, and prevent one set of people from becoming your own internal McCarthy Committee (aka Morals R Us).

2. Customers That Demand Truly Unreasonable Changes in Policy or Program

After all the talk throughout this book about listening and responding to your customers, after all the text that I have put in front of you about being flexible, now I am going to tell you to stop, think, and sometimes, put your foot down and say no. Why? Because there are times when your customers, even your best and biggest customers, will ask (or demand) that you do something that is outside of your organizational value set. This problem is closely related to the preceding first problem, the markets trying to move your organization away from its values. Here, though, the issue is a particular customer who wants something independent of larger market trends. Rather than being anonymous and monolithic, the demand becomes very local, very personal, and very, very difficult to refuse.

❏ **FOR EXAMPLE:** A client organization of mine that provides day care for children has a wonderful model of care that includes a great deal of hands-on activities, a lot of music, a low staff-to-child ratio and, after age three, community service. That's right, they take the kids out to pick up litter, rake senior citizens' lawns, clear tables at the local soup kitchen, wrap Christmas presents for needy children at the holidays, and so forth. No activity lasts more than about 15 minutes (these are, after all, three- and four-year-olds), but the idea is clear: Help other people when you can. The center has exceptional parent support and enthusiasm and tries to be affordable to all members of the community. About five years ago the director called me with a real dilemma: The major employer in the town of 70,000 people had approached the day care center inquiring whether the center would be interested in building and running a day care unit on the grounds of the company factory. The money being offered was excellent, profitable, and would allow the overall organization to offer more scholarships to low-income children. The company center would be available only to employees and their relatives, which was fine with the director. What bothered her were two requirements of the company: to raise the staff-to-child ratio—the extra staff were not "needed" according to the company—and a prohibition on community service work done by the children and staff, due to a decision by the corporate attorney that there was much too much liability associated with such events.

The director was really torn. The profits earned would allow more mission (in the form of scholarships) being provided to families who really needed it. But, she asked me, was she violating a core belief in order to get that money? In the best tradition of high-priced consultants everywhere, I avoided answering, and instead asked her what *she* thought. (Seriously, it is always better to help people figure out what *they* think rather than tell them what *you* think, at least if they have to follow through on the decision. The action then becomes theirs, rather than yours, and one that they will implement with determination.)

The director answered that she felt she would violate her organization's values, and she would not proceed with these stipulations to the contract. We then brainstormed on how to approach the company, to see if there was any room for negotiation. The director called her contact at the company and told him that she was fine with everything but the two conditions previously noted. She said that it should really not be a concern of the company what the staff-to-child ratio was as long as it was within licensing parameters, as the contract was a fixed amount per year. Further, she noted that the community service was integral to the organization's way of providing services, and that she would sign a waiver of liability for off-site trips, if that would help the company with its concerns.

The company answer? No, thanks. The director called me back disappointed, but resolute that she had made the right decision. Oh, the rest of the story had a happy ending. A week later the company called back, having been hounded by its employees to hire the day care center. The company agreed to let the center provide services as it wished, and the contract was signed within a week. But remember that when she made the decision to stand her ground, the director thought she was kissing the entire project goodbye.

☞ **HANDS ON:** Here is another time to use your staff. You have (or should have) a core set of procedures on how you provide your services. Those are based on a set of beliefs about what is best for the people you serve. It would behoove you to meet with your staff and figure out what parts, if any, of what you do are inviolate. Are there things that you just won't compromise on? Again, I don't want you to set your entire service array in concrete—then you would resist innovation and continuous improvement. But, to paraphrase George Bush, where is your line in the sand? Ask your staff.

3. Chasing Dollars Instead of Mission

Remember the diagram I showed you all the way back in Chapter 2, The Benefits of the Social Entrepreneurism Model, of the organization that had evolved from just doing outpatient counseling into providing transportation, day care, recreational services, residential services, and so forth? To refresh your memory, its organizational chart looked like Exhibit 12-1.

And, as I said in Chapter 2, there was no way that these good people had core competencies in all of these various industries when they started

Exhibit 12-1   Model organization chart.

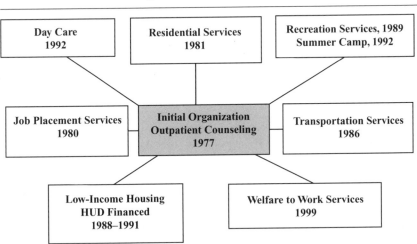

each new service. They learned on the job, and the funding climate of that time allowed them time to learn. As I have said repeatedly, times have changed, and you've got to be good at what you do, from day one.

The irony is that, in order to accommodate to the new environment, you and your organization are moving toward becoming more entrepreneurial, which tells you to focus on what markets want and what you can do well. By doing so, you run the risk of coming full circle and, again, just chasing dollars. Because for a competent, entrepreneurial organization, there are so, so many dollars to chase.

❏ **FOR EXAMPLE:** A great number of organizations that provide vocational services to adults with disabilities have developed a three-pronged continuum of service: They test the adults to see their initial capabilities, provide what is known as sheltered work for those unable to work in a normal integrated environment, and then work to train and place even people with severe disabilities in competitive employment. Some of these agencies even run what they consider temp agencies, which place both people with and without disabilities in jobs. All of this is well and good. But a recent trend concerns me greatly.

The advent of true welfare reform in the mid-1990s led to funds being available to help get people off of the welfare rolls and into jobs. Hundreds of not-for-profits that provide services to people with disabilities have applied for the funding on the assumption that finding a job for a person with a disability is a transferrable skill to finding a job for someone on welfare. I couldn't disagree more. This is classic money chasing and rationalizing that a competence is multifaceted. Most aren't.

☞ **HANDS ON:** As we've noted throughout the book, the sequence of decision is this:

1. Does doing this service support our mission?
2. Can I do this service *well* from day one?
3. Is there sufficient want in the community to merit my start-up costs?
4. What is the mission return on investment?
5. What is the financial return on investment?

Don't just chase the dollars. Remember that the outcome you need most is more high-quality mission, not just any mission for anybody, any place, any time! I know that for many organizations this is a very, very hard habit to break, but it needs to stop if you are to really achieve the status of social entrepreneur.

4. Going for Short-Term Returns Instead of Long-Term Gains

I've already told you that good social entrepreneurs have to think on two levels: the return on investment in mission, and the same return in money. In addition, they have to think on two separate time scales: short *and* long term. As you build your competencies and hone your business evaluation skills, there will be many, many opportunities for short-term returns, ones that provide services and dollars today, this week, month, quarter, or year. The danger is getting seduced by the vision of cash in the bank and services in the community in the near future, and forgetting to think about the resulting long-term impact on your organization's mission capability.

❏ **FOR EXAMPLE:** An affordable-housing organization that worked with residents to build or renovate housing in the Southwest had what it thought was a wonderful problem at the beginning of 1995: a possibility of tripling its output over the coming year. The chapter, which normally built two homes a year, had been approached by the family of a wealthy volunteer who had died with an offer to fund the costs associated with seven homes, but only if they were all up and occupied in 15 months. This organization was heavily volunteer-based, and this kind of growth would stretch the capabilities of this organization to the max.

The board met to consider its options. For tax reasons that don't bear going into (and that, frankly, I never did completely understand) the funds had to be donated and used within 15 months. The family, for additional reasons, would not contemplate a multiyear gift or the establishment of a trust. Nor would they agree to less than seven homes. It was an all-or-nothing opportunity. The board, after lengthy discussion, decided to go for it.

Despite nearly insurmountable obstacles, they got the houses built and properly occupied, the final one on the afternoon of the last day of the 15-month time line. So, the story had a happy ending, right? Think again. The burnout rate for the volunteers was extremely high. All but one of the board resigned in the next four months, recruitment of new volunteers lagged, and during the next four years (1996 through 1999) the total number of new homes built was two. Not two per year, but two for the four years. Thus, if you look at the numbers over a four-year period, the output of new homes fell, not rose. How so? If you projected the normal housing rate of two per year for the five years of 1995–1999, the organization would have built 10 homes. In reality, it got only nine built. And, the organization was much less mission-capable for the future.

☞ **HANDS ON:** The best single tool to help you avoid the short-term trap is to look at your strategic plan. Ask this: Does this new activity or action support a long-term goal or objective of our strategic plan? If so, fine, it probably will have a long-term positive impact. But if not, you need to ask what mission rationale there is for the idea, and whether the fact that it is not in the strategic plan is due to a significant change in your organization's situation, or is it just that you are thinking too short term? *Note:* If you don't have a strategic plan, you need one, and soon. The lack of such a plan indicates to me that you are thinking in short time frames rather than the longer horizons that good stewardship demands.

Please understand that there are often very valid reasons to pursue short-term outcomes. These might be such issues as a rapidly closing window of opportunity, a one-year funding cycle that will not repeat, a service request that comes with the guarantee of mission outcomes and large net revenue. But always assess the costs—the upheaval in your organization that often results from rapid change, the investment in time and money. Make sure that by helping your community now, you don't cripple your organization later on.

There are many ways to mess up a good thing, and social entrepreneurism is, surely, a good thing. The biggest danger is to forget the overall point of the entrepreneurism—producing more mission, making your organization stronger and more mission-capable. In the long run, the best way to avoid seduction is to evaluate business opportunities with your SE team and to make sure that your business evaluation criteria have some categories to assure that you aren't just chasing dollars, violating your core beliefs, or looking for a quick buck. That is not what SE is all about. Don't let the sirens lure you on to the rocks.

B. MAKING SURE THAT MISSION, NOT JUST MONEY, IS THE BOTTOM LINE

I'm sure the previous section brings up questions in your mind. Is there a trick to keeping on track? Is there some technique that can make it easy, or at least easier, to stay on course, always pursuing the mission? Is there an organizational compass that can keep us on course? Well, yes and no. There is a technique; it isn't hard, but it is work. The compass is your mission. But, as with any compass, to do you any good, you have to have it out and visible, and you have to check it regularly.

❏ **FOR EXAMPLE:** I am a private pilot, and fly a small, single-engine plane. I also love to sail, and my earliest recollection as a child is of sailing with my father. You might think that these two avocations are vastly different, one being in two dimensions while the other is in three, flying being (in my case) motorized, while sailors eschew being "under power" above all else. But both disciplines have the same rule: "Stop paying attention for *three seconds* and you are off course." You have to stay focused, you have to keep looking way out ahead to stay on course, avoid obstacles, and anticipate what happens next.

The same goes for you. You can easily be distracted by your entrepreneurial endeavors from the mission-based course you need to follow. You and your fellow managers have to keep focused on your mission and your organizational values. To do this, they have to be visible, and, as I said earlier in the book, be available on the table at your management, committee, and board meetings. The mission should be visible in everyone's office and be a tool for discussion in small groups and large meetings. Will it end all arguments? No, of course not, but it *will* keep you focused on the point, which is first, last, and always your mission.

❏ **FOR EXAMPLE:** A children's museum in the Midwest was faced with a choice between providing hands-on science exhibits in elementary schools and doing the preparatory work necessary to implement a capital fund drive that would, if successful, allow it to build a new building. The museum, which was seven years old, had always occupied rented space that had been renovated, and thus was adequate but not optimal for its needs. The capital fund drive would take a major effort of the staff and volunteers, and just as this effort was to begin, the local school board approached the museum with a request to provide services for a fee in the schools.

Here was a great opportunity, but also a huge time commitment. The design and development of portable displays that could be used in the schools would be a challenge. Both staff and volunteer resources would be taxed. Doing both projects was just not possible. It had to be one or the other.

A vexing choice to say the least. Should the museum provide services immediately and, as a result of the exposure in the schools, draw more families to the museum, or should it focus on getting a better space for *all* of the families that did visit the museum? The board and staff talked, and talked, and gnashed their collective teeth. They analyzed costs, looked at time lines, reviewed marketing information, all without coming to a consensus. Then someone suggested using the mission statement, which read: *"Provide an accessible, enjoyable, challenging, hands-on, science-based learning environment to children*

12 and under and their families." A board member noted that the evaluations that the museum had been collecting showed that the people that came to the museum felt that they already were getting an "accessible, enjoyable, challenging, and hands-on experience." In fact, 90 percent of people who came to the museum for the first time returned at least twice more. This board member then observed that the mission was already being met in the museum building, but not yet outside. This argument swayed the other board and staff members, even those who were really set on a new, even better space. The organization's board voted unanimously to defer the capital campaign for at least three years and to pursue the choice that made more mission sense first.

I didn't tell you the dollar side of the story: which choice would have made more money, because the real dilemma here was ego ("Hey look, we have our own building") for some of the board and staff versus mission. But by using their mission statement and resetting their compass, they did the right thing. They kept mission as their bottom line.

☞ **HANDS ON:** I have our organizational mission right over my computer monitor, where I see it every day when I sit back and ponder a particular problem. I know an exec who has turned his organization's mission statement into a moving screen saver and provided it to all staff who want it. The mission shows up on the computer screens after a few minutes of computer inactivity. I work with an organization where the mission is read and discussed before every single board meeting, much like a devotion before a church committee meeting. And there is the agency that has a $100 quarterly award to the staff person who most evidences the mission in daily work. All of these are ways of staying closer to the mission, more on course. What would work for your organization?

Mission is always the bottom line. No money, no mission, certainly, but decisions and investments *must* result in more mission, or at least more mission capability, to be appropriate.

C. FINAL THOUGHTS

Throughout this book, I have tried to translate the for-profit business world into the mission-based world you know so well, attempting to make the point that many traditional business methods can have good mission outcomes. As a result, it may well have seemed to you that I consider not-for-profits less educated, less enlightened than for-profits. Or that the learning curve is only in one direction: for-profits teaching not-for-profits. Not true.

In nearly 20 years of training and consulting with not-for-profits I have found universally bright, motivated, educated, committed people serving in both paid and volunteer roles. And, over and over, I have been told by board members that their for-profit employer could sure learn a lot from the not-for-profit sector in the areas of employee motivation and how to make do, improvise, and do a great deal with too few resources. Such improvisation is, of course, one of the seeds of entrepreneurism.

I often get e-mail from graduate students who are researching our field, and I recently answered an inquiry that listed a number of questions, one of which was this: "What do successful for-profits learn from not-for-profits?" That gave me a pause, and then the answer overwhelmed me with its obviousness: The best, most successful for-profits are on a mission, too. Just like you are. I know people who work for Federal Express, Land's End, Cisco, Microsoft, Marriott, and Disney. Those people and those organizations are unified by being on a common mission, not just on a quest for stock options. Excellent for-profits have learned from you, the not-for-profit sector, that mission motivates more than money. Remember that.

It is time for me to leave you and for you to proceed down the entrepreneurial path at your own pace using, I hope, at least some of the tools and ideas that I have shown you. Some readers may race toward entrepreneurism, quickly evaluating opportunities, discarding many, embracing others, all the while convincing their staff and board with near evangelistic zeal that becoming and remaining social entrepreneurs is the last best hope for their mission. Others readers may adopt the slow-lane approach, building their entrepreneurial capacity before beginning to look at mission-based market opportunities, or just dealing with current programs and funding in an entrepreneurial mode before leaping into the fray of a new product or service.

Some readers will try to go down the road alone, but most will find that they need to bring a team with them: their staff, board, volunteers, and at least some of their major funders. Some will find that their community openly and actively supports their entrepreneurial aspirations; others will find deep-seated opposition, resentment, and dismay.

The journey to entrepreneurism is never the same for any of us. And, once we arrive at the status of entrepreneur, there is no one waiting to award us a laurel, no medal we can wear, or diploma suitable for framing. Only we know it. Only individually can we look back at our work week, or month, or year, and say, "Yeah, we looked at all our options and made a good choice—for the right reasons. We took a chance, sure, but we did it based on the best information available." And, often, we can add, "And it sure worked out!" In other situations, we'll say, "And, while it didn't go as expected, we learned something. We'll know more the next time."

And there it is, there is the key phrase: *the next time.* For the true social entrepreneur, there is always a next time, a next venture, a next service, a next product, a next alliance, a next project, a next person to serve. Entrepreneurs are always looking for a way to leverage their organizations to greater mission output, always looking for a change in what the market wants that matches up with a core competence of the organization, always looking for reasonable risk to take on behalf of the people their organizations serve.

Social entrepreneurs can't rest on their accomplishments. They do learn from their experiences, but they don't spend a whole lot of time waiting for the next great idea to hit them on the head. They are out looking, asking, thinking, brainstorming, observing. There is always another person to help, another service to provide, another need to meet. This may sound like a lot of work, and it is. And it is significantly easier to do if everyone in your organization adopts an entrepreneurial mindset. But for a while, you may just have to go it alone or with just a small group of entrepreneurial peers.

Be assured, though, that others will join you, sooner or later. Why? Because the tenets of entrepreneurism are the way that not-for-profits will succeed in meeting the needs of their communities and the wants of their funders. The ideas of risk taking, careful business planning, mission-based marketing, and seeking constant customer satisfaction will, in the end, provide both more organizational success and more mission out the door. Others will see that and join you in your quest.

In 1985, I gave a speech to a group of 300 not-for-profit managers, and I said the following: "Profit, in a not-for-profit, is not only legal, allowable, and ethical, it is *essential* for the organization's continued success. For without profit, there is no money for innovation, and without innovation, an organization withers on the vine. Call it what you will, but profit is not a dirty word." I was booed loudly that day; someone actually threw a pencil at me from the crowd. No one thought much about innovation or flexibility in those days. They just wanted a return to pre-Reagan funding levels.

By 1990, I had helped over 200 not-for-profit organizations start profitable businesses, ones that enhanced their mission. Not-for-profit leaders had gotten the message that they were on their own and needed to try something new. By 1995, I was spending nearly all of my consulting time helping organizations with mergers, alliances, and collaborations, as the best and brightest not-for-profit managers in many communities raced to keep ahead of changes in funding, new models of service, and the demands of their constituencies for higher quality and lower cost.

In 2000, the idea of a not-for-profit making money is quite widely accepted. The idea of a 501(c)(3) as a not-for-profit *business* no longer draws gasps of dismay, but rather almost universal nods of agreement, if not yawns of boredom—it's old news. The old model of the charity is long gone—and may it rest in peace. The new, well, not so new any longer, but certainly the most-effective model of not-for-profits is that of the social entrepreneur. Just as communism was irreversibly vanquished by capitalism in the Cold War, so the idea of the nice, kind, but weak charity has been irrevocably pushed out the door by the compassionate, socially concerned, entrepreneurial not-for-profit. Mission has become a business, and our communities have benefitted from it.

There is no going back. Governments, corporate donors, foundations, and even United Ways have found that funding strong, businesslike organizations makes sense, because it results in more and better mission for less money. So does offering risk-and-reward kinds of funding. Such methods of purchasing services allow more accurate evaluation and measurement of outcomes and can be explained and rationalized to taxpayers, donors, stockholders, and the community.

So, as you finish this book and return to the challenges facing you, the question is, what will you do now? I hope that your answer is, "Help my organization learn how to become and stay entrepreneurial."

I hope that is your answer, because if it is, your community will reap the benefits, and your organization will be there to assure that it does. If that isn't your answer . . .

RECAP

In this final chapter, I provided you with some cautions regarding social entrepreneurism and the danger that it poses of distracting you from your mission. In the first part of the chapter, I showed you how to stay close to your mission, citing four key ways that you can be enticed to veer from the straight and narrow. These were the following:

1. Markets that move outside of your values envelope
2. Customers that demand truly unreasonable changes in policy or program
3. Chasing dollars instead of mission
4. Going for short-term returns instead of long-term gains

I also showed you how to combat these threats to your mission continuity. Then, we turned to ways to assure that mission, not just money, is always the bottom line for your organization.

Finally, I gave you one last reality check, emphasizing that entrepreneurism is the management model that will most enable your mission-based organization to succeed in today's significantly different environment.

Social entrepreneurism works. It can provide you with the tools to make better mission-based policy, planning, financial, and service decisions. It can provide you with a framework with which to weigh your investments and measure the mission as well as the financial return on those investments. I hope you believe that now and are willing to make the choice to pursue entrepreneurism. It is not without risk, but hasn't that been the theme of this book? And that's my last piece of advice: Take a reasonable risk on behalf of the people your organization serves, and become a social entrepreneur. Good luck.

Peter C. Brinckerhoff
Springfield, Illinois
March 2000

QUESTIONS FOR DISCUSSION: CHAPTER 12

1. Do we use our mission and values enough in our decisions to grow or to retain certain services? How can we involve the mission more?

2. Do we have an up-to-date set of core values to rely on? If not, how can we develop and publicize them?

3. Do we chase the dollars? Why? How can we avoid it?

4. What is our next step to becoming social entrepreneurs? How do we stay entrepreneurs for the long haul?

Resources for Further Study

OVERVIEW

In this section you will find references for print resources, organizations, and Web sites that may help you as you further your study of social entrepreneurism.

A. PRINT RESOURCES

Papers

Dees, J. Gregory, "The Meaning of Social Entrepreneurship," 1998, The Kauffman Center for Entrepreneurial Leadership, Stanford University.

Emerson, Jed, "The U.S. Nonprofit Capital Market," 1998, The Roberts Foundation Enterprise Development Fund.

Books

Boschee, Jer. 1998. *Merging Mission and Money: A Board Member's Guide to Social Entrepreneurship.* National Center for Nonprofit Boards: Washington, D.C.

Skloot, Edward. 1995. *The Nonprofit Entrepreneur.* Foundation Center: New York.

Zack, Gerald. 1998. *The Unrelated Business Income Tax.* Nonprofit Resource Center: San Francisco.

B. ORGANIZATIONS

Ashoka

Ashoka is a global not-for-profit organization that identifies and supports social entrepreneurs with innovative solutions to social problems in their countries. It sponsors fellowships throughout the world in effecting social change and has an interesting view on social entrepreneurship.

> Ashoka
> Innovators for the Public
> 1700 North Moore Street
> Suite 1920
> Arlington, VA 22209
> Tel: (703) 527-8300
> Fax: (703) 527-8383
> E-mail: info@ashoka.org
> Web site: www.ashoka.org

Roberts Enterprise Development Fund

A function of the Roberts Foundation, the Enterprise Development Fund's goal is to assist not-for-profit groups in achieving both increased scale and full sustainability in the marketplace. In addition, the Fund networks on a national level with others who fund and/or execute nonprofit enterprise strategies. The Fund is committed to providing informational support to those seeking assistance regarding nonprofit enterprise. The Web site *www.redf.org/* includes good resources including a FAQ and a listing of current not-for-profit businesses. Links to other organizations are also provided.

> Roberts Enterprise Development Fund
> Presidio Building 1009, First Floor
> P.O. Box 29266,
> San Francisco, CA 94129-0266

National Center for Social Entrepreneurs

The National Center for Social Entrepreneurs is a not-for-profit organization founded in 1985, and the International Centre for Social Entrepreneurs is a wholly owned subsidiary. The mission of both organizations is to encourage entrepreneurship throughout the not-for-profit sector and to help individual not-for-profits think and act in an entrepreneurial manner.

> The National Center for Social Entrepreneurs
> The International Centre for Social Entrepreneurs
> Bassett Creek Office Plaza
> Suite 310
> 5801 Duluth Street
> Minneapolis, MN 55422
> Tel: (612) 595-0890

Toll-free: (800) 696-4066
Fax: (612) 595-0232
E-mail: ncse@socialentrepreneurs.org
Web site: www.socialentrepreneurs.org

C. WEB SITES

Note: Listing Web sites is fraught with the danger that, by the time you read this, the site will have moved or been discontinued. I have tried to limit my listings to organizations that I believe will stay on the Web. If the URL listed does not exist when you read this, search for the sponsoring organization. If organizations previously listed have Web sites, they are listed with the organization.

Social Entrepreneur Site

This site is run by Dr. Swapan Garain, a professor in India who wants to promote social entrepreneurism. The site includes some not-for-profit resources and some research underway, among other items of interest.

http://members.tripod.com/~swapan_garain/

Sample Business Plans

This site keeps a set of free business plans for you to review and to use as benchmarks for your own. It also has free marketing plans and some tools to help you match your needs with its samples.

www.bplans.com/start.cfm

CEO Express

I love the following site, as it has links to everything I need. You can find information on financing, the SBA, competitive mortgage and equipment financing, business development groups, and more all in one place. A great site!

www.ceoexpress.com/

Wiley Nonprofit Resource Center

This Web site features:

- A nonprofit catalog where you can order and search for titles online. View book and author information about management, law/tax, fundraising, accounting, and finance titles.

- A threaded discussion forum, which will provide you and your colleagues with the chance to ask questions, share knowledge, and debate issues important to your organization and the sector.
- Over 500 free forms and worksheets to help run any nonprofit organization more efficiently and effectively. Forms are updated monthly to cover a new key area of nonprofit management.
- Useful links to many nonprofit resources online.

The Wiley Nonprofit Series brings together an extraordinary team of experts in the fields of nonprofit management, fund-raising, law, accounting, and finance. This Web site highlights new books, which present the best, most innovative practices being used in the nonprofit sector today. It also highlights established works, which through their use in the day-to-day operations of thousands of nonprofits, have proven themselves to be invaluable to any nonprofit looking to raise more money or improve its operations while still remaining in compliance with all rules and regulations.

For nearly 200 years, Wiley has prided itself on being a publisher of books known for thoroughness, rigor, and readability. Please browse the Web site. You are sure to find valued titles that you need to navigate the new world of nonprofit action.

www.wiley.com/nonprofit

Index

Until very recently, popular belief held that business skills were not needed at charitable organizations. No longer. Far from interfering with an organization's ability to provide needed services, techniques such as marketing, cash flow analysis, property management, and good use of technology all contribute to a charitable organization's mission capability. Unlike a not-for-profit that thinks of itself as a charity, the successful not-for-profit is really a mission-based business. In an era of rapid change, increasing competition, and the need for more accountability to governments, foundations, insurers, and donors, knowing how to innovate, compete, and take reasonable risks on behalf of the mission is critical. It is, in short, the era of the social entrepreneur.

Skilled social entrepreneurs have the ability to get the most mission out of the resources at hand—including traditional business techniques. Finally, here is a book that will help you learn their techniques. In *Social Entrepreneurship*, you will learn how successful social entrepreneurs:

☆ Focus on community wants and needs

☆ Match those with core competencies to provide the highest quality services

☆ Assess risk and gauge opportunity

☆ Develop new project ideas and test their feasibility

☆ Write a business plan

☆ Project finances in the plan

☆ Tap into new sources of funding

☆ Develop the idea of social entrepreneurship throughout the organization

☆ Make sure that *mission,* not money, is the bottom line

Also included are the seven essential steps of the not-for-profit business development process, real-world case studies, sample business plans, and a self-assessment process to determine if your organization is ready for social entrepreneurism. In addition to entrepreneurs, middle managers, policy setters, volunteers, and a host of other important staff members will get value from the mission-beneficial information in this book. Most important, *Social Entrepreneurship* will help you to help your organization succeed and thrive—and make your job more interesting and productive.

PETER C. BRINCKERHOFF is an internationally acclaimed consultant, author, and lecturer. He is President of Corporate Alternatives, inc., the consulting firm that he founded in 1982. He is a former staff member, executive director, board member, and volunteer for local, state, and national not-for-profit organizations. He lives in Springfield, Illinois.